What Every
Principal
Needs to Know About
Special
Education

P9-DZY-295

We would like to dedicate this book to all of the principals who work so tirelessly to ensure that every student receives a world-class education.

What Every
Principal
Needs to Know About
Special
Education

Margaret J. McLaughlin \ Victor Nolet

CORWIN PRESS
A Sage Publications Company
Thousand Oaks, California

Copyright © 2004 by Corwin Press

All rights reserved. When forms and sample documents are included, their use is authorized only by educators, local school sites, and/or noncommercial entities who have purchased the book. Except for that usage, no part of this book may be reproduced or utilized in any form or by any means, electronic or mechanical, including photocopying, recording, or by any information storage and retrieval system, without permission in writing from the publisher.

For information:

Corwin Press
A Sage Publications Company
2455 Teller Road
Thousand Oaks, California 91320
www.corwinpress.com

Sage Publications Ltd.
6 Bonhill Street
London EC2A 4PU
United Kingdom

Sage Publications India Pvt. Ltd.
B-42, Panchsheel Enclave
Post Box 4109
New Delhi 110 017 India

Printed in the United States of America

Library of Congress Cataloging-in-Publication Data

McLaughlin, Margaret J.
What every principal needs to know about special education / Margaret J. McLaughlin, Victor Nolet.
    p. cm.
Includes bibliographical references and index.
ISBN 0-7619-3830-3 (cloth) — ISBN 0-7619-3831-1 (pbk.)
    1. Special education-United States-Administration. 2. Children with disabilities-Education-United States. 3. School principals-United States.
I. Nolet, Victor. II. Title
LC4019.15.M178 2004
371.9—dc22

2003021251

This book is printed on acid-free paper.

05   06   10 9 8 7 6 5 4 3

Acquisitions Editor:	Robert D. Clouse
Editorial Assistant:	Jingle Vea
Production Editor:	Denise Santoyo
Copy Editor:	Toni Williams
Typesetter:	C&M Digitals (P) Ltd.
Indexer:	Kathy Paparchontis
Cover Designer:	Tracy E. Miller
Graphic Designer:	Lisa Miller

Contents

Acknowledgments

We want to acknowledge the incredible organization and persistence of Valerie Foster, who was able to create a whole from our many parts. We thank you for your patience.

Also, we acknowledge and thank Robb Clouse for his persistence and guidance throughout the development of this book.

Finally we would like to acknowledge the support and encouragement of our respective spouses Stan and Geneva, our chief collaborators.

Corwin Press gratefully acknowledges the contributions of the following reviewers:

Debbie Toy
Principal
Trail Wind Elementary School
Boise, ID

Bob Algozzine
Professor, Author
University of North Carolina
College of Education
Charlotte, NC

Carl Lashley
Professor, Author
University of North Carolina at
Greensboro
Educational Leadership and
Cultural Foundations
Greensboro, NC

Darryl L. Williams
Principal
William H. Farquhar
Middle School
Olney, MD

James C. Brown
Assistant Executive Director
Massachusetts Elementary School
Principals Association
Marlborough, MA

Deborah Gartland
Assistant Professor, Towson
University
Reading, Special Education, and
Instructional Technology
Towson, MD

Festus E. Obiakor
Professor, Author
University of Wisconsin
Milwaukee, WI

Maureen Stamoulis
Principal
Cashell Elementary School
Rockville, MD

Maureen Keyes
Professor, Author
University of Wisconsin–
Milwaukee
Department of Exceptional
Education
Milwaukee, WI

Joseph Staub
Teacher
Thomas Starr King Middle School
Los Angeles, CA

Anne Jordan
Professor
Department of Curriculum,
Teaching, and Learning
OISE/University of Toronto
Toronto, Ontario
CANADA

Jennifer Prue
Professor
University of Vermont
College of Education
Burlington, VT

David P. Riley
Executive Director
Urban Special Education
Leadership Collaborative
Education Development Center, Inc.
Newton, MA

Kathleen McLane
Senior Director
Publications and
Continuing Education
The Council for Exceptional Children
Reston, VA

Stephen Bugaj
Superintendent of Schools
Cameron City School District
Emporium, PA

About the Authors

Margaret J. McLaughlin is Professor of Special Education in the Department of Special Education and Associate Director of the Institute for the Study of Exceptional Children and Youth at the University of Maryland, College Park.

She has been involved in special education all of her professional career, beginning as a teacher of students with serious emotional and behavior disorders and learning disabilities. She conducts research investigating educational reform and students with disabilities, including how students with disabilities are accessing standards and the impact of high stakes accountability on students with disabilities. She has consulted with numerous national, state, and local agencies and organizations on issues related to students with disabilities and the impact of standards-driven reform policies. She teaches graduate courses in disability policy and has written extensively in the area of school reform and students with disabilities.

Victor Nolet is Director of Assessment and Evaluation for the Woodring College of Education at Western Washington University. In this role, he is responsible for evaluation of teacher education and professional programs in the college. He earned his doctorate in special education from the University of Oregon in 1992, specializing in classroom-based assessment and evaluation.

He has published numerous research articles, monographs, and book chapters and coauthored books about data-based decision making and evaluation of student outcomes. His recent work has focused on analysis of the effects of national accountability and assessment policy on school outcomes for students with disabilities. He is a Senior Research Consultant for the Educational Policy Reform Research Institute, and he frequently teaches courses in evaluation, assessment, and educational research.

What Every Principal Needs to Know About Special Education

This book is different from many that have been developed for principals on the topic of special education. It is different in that it does not solely focus on describing *the law* and special education rules and procedures. Rather, this book is designed as a guidebook to developing strong school leaders who "are strong educators, anchoring their work on central issues of learning and teaching and school improvement" (Interstate School Leaders Licensure Consortium [ISLLC], 1996, p. 5).

A building principal, who is a school leader, is critical to creating effective special education services. In today's climate of high standards and high stakes accountability, every school principal needs to understand the foundations of effective special education. Principals need to know about special education because they are responsible for ensuring that students with disabilities perform well on assessments. More important, when special education is working, when parents and families feel confident about their child's education, it is because a strong, supportive, and informed building principal has created a school that values educating every child.

Delegating responsibility for special education to special education teachers was never good leadership. But, until recently it was possible for a principal to leave programmatic decisions to the special educators. Today, no principal can abdicate responsibility for any group of students, including those who receive special education. The expectations for public schools have never been higher than they are today, and at no time have schools been under such close public scrutiny. Schools exist in a rapidly changing policy and funding environment that demands new skills and knowledge from principals. The case of Mr. Baker illustrates this point.

Mr. Baker has been a principal for 8 years, first as an elementary school principal and for the past 3 years within a middle school of 850 students. Mr. Baker is proud of his school and his students and staff. Of his 850 sixth, seventh, and eighth graders, 47% receive free and reduced meals. He has more students who qualify, but the families just don't apply. Also, 12% of his students have individualized education plans (IEPs). Since he came to this middle school, the test scores in reading and writing and math have increased by about 20-50%. This comes after several years of flat or declining scores. Faculty turnover has decreased. Last year, he had to replace only five teachers, and the school staff is, in Mr. Baker's opinion, really starting to work together as a team.

But, this past school year something happened to change Mr. Baker's opinion of his school. Last fall, Mr. Baker received the disaggregated test scores and attendance rates for specific groups of students, including those with disabilities. While Mr. Baker was aware of how his low-income students had been progressing and how African American and Hispanic students were doing as a group, he had never looked at his students with disabilities. His assistant principal, Ms. Gregor, and his lead special education teacher, Mr. Rich, were responsible for these students. The school hadn't had any problems with parents; no formal complaints had been filed. Mr. Baker thought things were OK.

Mr. Baker is about to find out that there are a number of things he now needs to know, starting with just who the students with disabilities in his school are and what he is expected to accomplish with them. Mr. Baker, like many of his peers, has entered a new era in public education. He is now expected to be a school leader for *all* students and programs and to be accountable for improving achievement of *all* students in his school. These responsibilities require Mr. Baker and his peers to gain new knowledge about special education: both new legal requirements as well as new ideas about what special education should look like in a school. The new knowledge includes having an understanding of how to reduce unnecessary referrals and identification, how to provide access to the general education curriculum, and how to create a collaborative culture between general and special educators and a whole school commitment to the achievement of every student. It will require Mr. Baker to also understand and interpret the data pertaining to students with disabilities and to act on those data.

In summary, it will require understanding the concepts presented in this book.

This book provides basic foundational knowledge of special education that every principal needs in order to lead effectively. Section I provides an overview of critical elements of the special education policy framework. Section II presents the foundations of a quality special education program and Section III gives you practical guidance in how to create effective special education. Section IV summarizes the information and skills you will need to help you develop a clear vision for your own school.

FIVE THINGS EVERY PRINCIPAL NEEDS TO KNOW ABOUT SPECIAL EDUCATION

Principals who are effective leaders of special education need to understand five key principles.

1. Principals must understand the core special education legal foundations or *entitlements*. They should understand the underlying intent or rationale behind specific procedures. Following rules that have little meaning leads to cookie-cutter programs and pro forma compliance and not to effective special education. Principals who understand the legal foundations of special education are able to make the critical distinction between a student with a disability who is eligible to receive special education and one who is not.

2. Principals need to understand that effective special education matches instruction to the learning characteristics of students with disabilities. Neither disability labels nor categories provide the information necessary to create that match.

3. Principals must understand that special education is not a *place* nor a *program*. At the level of the school, special education is a set of services and supports that is provided to individual students to give them access to curriculum and to ensure that they continually learn and progress in that curriculum.

4. Principals must know how to meaningfully include students with disabilities in assessments and new accountability systems.

5. Principals need to know how to create the schoolwide conditions that support effective special education. Special education does not exist in a vacuum within a school. It has never been more important for principals to integrate special education into all aspects of the school and to ensure that efforts to improve schools fully include special education.

In the following sections, we expand on these key ideas. We provide specific knowledge and practical strategies, as well as examples for how to create effective special education. We hope you enjoy this book—we enjoyed writing it. We also hope you find it useful. We have spent countless hours in schools observing and working with special and general education teachers and we have been amazed by the knowledge and commitment of individual principals. Good special education exists in schools with caring, knowledgeable, and strong school leaders. Countless interviews with parents and teachers have shown us how a principal has made a difference to their school or with their child. Because of the difference you can make for children with disabilities, we hope that you find the ideas and resources in this book valuable.

Understanding the Basics of Special Education

Key Ideas for Section I

➢ Students who receive special education are a very diverse group. A large number of these students share many characteristics with other groups of students who have learning or behavior problems.

➢ Special education in a school is a *system* of supports and services; it is not a separate program or place.

➢ Special education policies and practices can vary tremendously from state to state and district to district, but the core principles remain consistent.

The Individuals With Disabilities Education Act, or IDEA, is the federal law that governs special education. The federal law is a combination of both civil rights statutes and educational laws. The law has three core requirements:

- All children with disabilities who need special education must be provided a *free, appropriate public education*, or FAPE.
- Each child's special education must be designed on an individual basis to meet his or her unique needs and must be provided in the *least restrictive environment*, or LRE.
- The rights of every child and youth with a disability and his or her family must be ensured and protected through procedural safeguards.

SOME FREQUENTLY ASKED
QUESTIONS ABOUT SPECIAL EDUCATION

Special education includes both *specially designed instruction* that meets the unique needs of a child or youth with a disability and *related services.* The IDEA defines what constitutes a related service. These services include transportation and other corrective and supportive services such as speech and language, physical therapy, and technology that an individual student may need to benefit from special education. Every student with a disability who is eligible for special education is entitled to receive a free and appropriate public education, meaning *specifically designed instruction* and related services as defined through the *individualized education program,* or IEP, which is a written document for a child developed by a team of professionals.

How Do We Know What Is an Appropriate Education?

This is a very interesting and difficult question. The IDEA and the courts define *appropriate* as education that has been provided in accordance with a child's IEP and is "reasonably calculated to confer benefit." The law assumes that a team of professionals, including a child's parents or guardian, is in the best position to determine what is appropriate for an individual student with a disability. Specific membership of an IEP team, as well as its content, procedures, and timelines, is determined by a combination of federal and state laws and local district procedures.

The IEP is central to special education. It is the official record of a child's legal entitlement to FAPE. Therefore, the procedures and paperwork surrounding the IEP more often reflect the legal nature of this document and not its original instructional purpose. As we write this book, Congress is considering changing some of the procedures surrounding the IEP. Among the changes being considered are extending the IEP reviews from one to three years and removing the requirements for short-term objectives. However, core principles of the IEP will remain:

- The IEP is to be developed by a *team* for an individual student with a disability.
- The IEP must be based on a careful assessment of the student's current level of performance in the general curriculum and the impact of that student's disability on his or her ability to progress in that curriculum.
- The IEP must clearly indicate what the student is expected to learn and be able to do and how this will be assessed.

What Is the Least Restrictive Environment?

This is another good question and one that has been subject to a lot of controversy over the years. The IDEA requires that children with disabilities be educated with nondisabled children to "the maximum extent appropriate." The regulations governing the IDEA also require that each district make available a continuum of placements as part of meeting the LRE requirement. These placements include regular classrooms, special classrooms, special schools, home instruction, and instruction in hospitals and institutions. The placements do not have to be used, but must be available should an IEP team determine that a specific student requires that setting.

The basic legal standard for determining the LRE is that each student's IEP team will determine what constitutes the least restrictive environment for that student. The decision requires that consideration first be given to providing special education and related services in the *regular* classroom. Education would only be provided in a more restrictive setting if it cannot be achieved with the use of a variety of aids and services within the regular classroom. A student cannot be educated outside of the regular classroom simply because of the nature of his or her disability, his or her educational needs, or the types of services he or she may require. We will talk more about LRE later in this section.

Are There Other Federal Disability Laws?

There are several other federal laws that provide important protections to children and adults with disabilities in public schools. Two of the major laws are Section 504 of the Vocational Rehabilitation Act and the Americans With Disabilities Act (ADA). Section 504 prohibits discrimination of persons with disabilities in all federally supported programs. It is broader than IDEA both in terms of which students are covered under the law and in that both public and private schools that receive any federal money are affected. The ADA is a comprehensive civil rights law that protects persons with disabilities in employment, public services and public accommodations, transportation, and telecommunications. Table 1.1 presents a comparison of key features of the three laws.

Several programs established under the Social Security Act (SSA) that are administered by individual states are also available to some children with disabilities. These include Medicaid (medical insurance), State Children's Health Insurance Program (medical insurance), and Supplemental Security Income (SSI), which

> For a quick introduction to these programs visit the Social Security Administration Web site: www.hcfa.gov.

Table 1.1   A Comparison of Three Federal Disability Laws

	ADA	SECTION 504	PART B OF IDEA
Definition of Disability	An individual with a disability is one who has a physical or mental impairment, has a record of such an impairment, or is regarded by others as having such an impairment. The impairment must substantially limit a major life activity.	Section 504 is nearly identical to ADA.	A child aged 3–21 who has been evaluated according to IDEA regulations and has mental retardation, a hearing impairment including deafness, a speech or language impairment, a visual impairment including blindness, emotional disturbance, an orthopedic impairment, autism, traumatic brain injury, another health impairment, a specific learning disability, deaf-blindness, or multiple disabilities *and who, because of the disability, needs special education and related services.* In some states, children ages 3–9 may be identified as having developmental delays. Children who require only related services and not special education are not eligible under the IDEA.
Eligibility	To be covered under the law, a person must meet the ADA's definition of a disability (and be qualified for the program, service, or job in the case of employment).	Section 504 is the same as the ADA. Students who have a disability that does not have an adverse impact on their ability to learn but may require special accommodation in order to access education may have individual accommodation plans.	A student must have a disability and must need special education and related services because of that disability in order to benefit from education.
Funding	No funding through the ADA.	No funding through Section 504.	Funds are provided to state education agencies that must "flow" the funds to local districts. States may devise their own formula for allocating federal (and state) special education funds.

provides payments to families of children under 18 who meet specific criteria of physical or mental impairment.

UNDERSTANDING THE DIFFERENCE BETWEEN FEDERAL, STATE, AND LOCAL SPECIAL EDUCATION REQUIREMENTS

"The law requires that we do this!" This is a frequent statement made by principals, teachers, and parents. Your first response to this should be to understand *which law* and to be sure that what you are doing is required by law and not simply a local practice or convention. Special education requirements in schools represent a complex mix of federal and special education laws and regulations, and local policies, practices, and tradition. Federal law holds state education agencies (SEAs) accountable for ensuring that the basic provisions and intents of the IDEA are met. The SEAs delegate responsibility to local districts to implement all legal procedures and rely on local districts to set policies and monitor practices. This delegation of responsibility results in a lot of variability across states, local districts, and schools as to who receives special education, meaning how eligibility is determined, as well as where and how special education and related services are provided and what procedures must be followed.

When a principal or teacher complains about burdensome paperwork and points to IEPs with double-digit pages, the first response is to blame federal law. Federal law defines what must be considered in the IEP, but SEAs or local districts develop the IEP forms and procedures. Very often, IEP forms have evolved from specific compliance issues in a district or state or a legal discussion. That is not to say that a principal can ignore these state or local policies, but a school leader needs to understand what is behind those forms. What is the legal standard or intent behind the form? What must be achieved in the document?

Before you decide to exercise any discretion over the design of a student's IEP and special education and related services, *make sure you know what a good program of special education and related services should include.* Remember, special education law is intended to protect the rights of individual students with disabilities and their families. When a dispute with a parent becomes adversarial, incorrect paperwork and procedures can become a school or district's Achilles' heel. Good procedures are important. Good services are even more important. We will discuss the IEP in more detail in Section II.

WHO IS ELIGIBLE FOR SPECIAL EDUCATION?

The IDEA requires that a child have a comprehensive and individual multidisciplinary evaluation before he or she receives special education or related services. Again, IDEA relies on multidisciplinary teams to establish a child's eligibility and requires a number of procedures that protect the child and parent in the assessment process.

Box 1.1   Identifying a Child for Special Education Is a Two-Pronged Decision

1. The child must first be determined to have a disability in one of the categories specified in IDEA.
2. The child must have a need for "special" education because of the disability. This assumes that well-designed general education instructional interventions are not sufficient for the child to receive an appropriate education.

Some children with documented disabilities may require only accommodations and not special education or related services. However, these students still are protected under Section 504 and the ADA. Just because a student has a disability doesn't necessarily make him or her eligible for special education under IDEA.

Procedures for determining eligibility for special education resulted from a long history within schools of placing certain students, notably minority students, poor students, and non-English-speaking students into special education classes without parental permission or knowledge. Often, children could be removed from general education solely based on the judgment of a teacher or principal.

CURRENT ISSUES IN ELIGIBILITY

One of the biggest changes in special education over the years since the passage of the federal special education law is in the numbers and characteristics of students who have been identified to receive special education and related services. Currently, federal law specifies 13 categories of disabilities that are eligible to receive special education. However, the vast majority of students in special education are classified in only four of those categories: learning disabilities, speech and language impairment, mental retardation, and emotional disturbance. (States and districts may choose other labels for these categories.)

According to annual reports issued by the Department of Education, the number of children receiving special education in the United States grew from 3.7 million in 1977 to 6.2 million during the 2000 school year. This number has grown each year. The largest increase has been in the category of learning disabilities, which has increased from about 1% of all students to close to 7% today. Autism is another category that grew from 54,000 to 65,000 in 1 year, a 21% increase.

Why Are the Numbers Increasing?

Research suggests that, in part, increases in the identification rates for some groups of students with disabilities are due to new, more refined diagnostic criteria and research into learning and behavior. Examples are new diagnostic criteria defining autism. However, there is also considerable evidence that a sizable number of students currently classified as having a disability instead have dyspedagogia, a history of inadequate instruction most notably in reading and language arts or math, or have not had basic behavioral supports or social adjustments.

Students who receive special education are a very heterogeneous group. Over the years, special educators have found that classifying students by disability is not particularly useful. Instead, we find that it is more useful to think of the students in terms of what types of instructional accommodations and modifications they require as evidenced by their learning. This research is leading to new ways of considering a student's eligibility for special education.

PREVENTING UNNECESSARY REFERRALS AND IDENTIFICATION

One new model for thinking about eligibility for special education, specifically for students who do not have a clear and apparent developmental or medically defined disability, is based on how a student responds to a

---

If you are interested in getting a sense of some of the differences that exist across states, take a look at the *Annual Report to Congress on the Implementation of the Individuals With Disabilities Education Act.* These annual reports are required by law and provide an indication of some of the important trends over the 25 years since the first federal special education law, PL 94-142, was passed. Some of the biggest changes have been in the numbers of students who are receiving special education and the increasing amounts of time these children and youths are spending in general education classrooms.

carefully planned and implemented set of instructional interventions. The model is based on several facts that are grounded in research conducted primarily with young children who experienced difficulty learning to read.

The vast majority of students with mild or high incidence disabilities, such as learning disabilities, mild mental retardation, and emotional disturbance, is identified only after the students have been in school for several years and have a history of achievement problems. Failure to progress in the curriculum is the symptom that most often prompts regular education teachers or parents to seek evaluations to determine the cause of the poor achievement. Those achievement difficulties are most often in reading, followed by math, and are compounded by social and behavioral problems.

Research in special education has consistently demonstrated the fallibility of labels and disability classifications either in explaining poor achievement or in determining which instruction the student needs to improve his or her learning. Elaborate diagnostic evaluations, including IQ tests, do not result in an instructional plan, nor are they sensitive enough to be able to monitor the effects of instruction. We also know that the earlier we, as educators, intervene with a learning or behavioral problem, the better.

Research suggests that a much more straightforward approach to identifying a student for special education is to consider a student eligible only after a set of increasingly intense instructional interventions are tried *by general and special education teachers within general education.* This approach requires that teachers assess precisely which skills and background knowledge (in the general education curriculum) the student has. Then, the student is provided small group instruction focused on those skills each day or several days a week over a very concentrated period of time. Teachers must carefully and continuously monitor whether the student is making progress. If he or she is not, the amount of instruction time or practice should be increased or the student may receive one-on-one instruction by paraprofessionals, adult volunteers, or peer tutors. Teachers continue to assess the student's progress, as well as how the tutor is implementing the intervention. Research indicates that only a few students may not respond to the focused and intensive instruction. These students are the ones who should be referred to special education and who will likely require long-term learning support.

Minority Students and Special Education

One of the most difficult issues educators have faced over the years has been the overrepresentation of minority students in special education. While white students make up almost two-thirds of all those receiving special education, 20% of the students are African American and 14% are Hispanic. Almost 3% of all African American students are classified as mentally retarded and about 1.5% are classified as emotionally disturbed as compared to about 1% of all white students. Almost 7% of white, African American, and Hispanic students are classified as having learning disabilities. These are national averages and mark the great variation from state to state and district to district. Research that has examined the relationship between race and special education using state- and district-level incidence data consistently confirms that African American students are about two and a half times more likely than white students to be identified as eligible for special education. Yet, controlled research studies investigating children with reading difficulties have found no differences in the incidence between white students and those from other racial or cultural groups.

The two categories of disability that account for most of the disproportionate representation are mild, or *educable*, mental retardation and emotional disturbance. This has led to the conclusion that the problem of overrepresentation is a combination of bias in the referral and initial diagnostic evaluation process and lack of appropriate instruction and support in classrooms.

> Research that has examined the relationship between identification rates in special education and the demographic and economic features of a school district or individual student has found that the odds for African American students being identified as either having mild mental retardation or emotional disturbance relate to district and student economic factors. Specifically, Oswald and his colleagues in the Civil Rights Project (Oswald, Coutinho, & Best, 2002) found that identification of African American students as having emotional disturbance was higher in wealthier districts.
>
> For more in-depth information, see the National Research Council report Web site, www.nas.edu/nrc, and the Civil Rights Project Web site, www.civilrightsproject.harvard.edu.

Both the U.S. Office of Civil Rights and the U.S. Department of Education are concerned about the overidentification of African American and Hispanic students in special education. Requirements for determining eligibility for special education are focusing more on using curriculum-based assessments to measure a student's educational performance and to deemphasize IQ and other psychological and traditional tests. The IDEA requires that "a group of qualified professionals and the parent of the child" must make the diagnosis of a disability and the school must share with the parent all reports and information documenting the disability.

These procedures are designed to protect minority children from being inappropriately placed in special education. However, most experts agree that the solution rests in more effective general education classroom instruction and support to teachers. In other words, preventing learning and behavior problems is much more effective than trying to ameliorate them later on.

Where Are Students With Disabilities Being Educated?

The concept of educating students with disabilities in the least restrictive environment is based on the belief that people with even the most significant disabilities should be fully integrated into communities, schools, and workplaces and should experience all of the typical routines of daily living. Over 30 years ago, many states or local districts had laws that restricted hundreds of thousands of children with disabilities from attending public schools. Over 200,000 children and youths with disabilities were housed in institutions. Other children were considered uneducable and sent home. Those students with disabilities fortunate enough to be allowed to enroll in school were often educated in separate classrooms or buildings with very separate curricula. Furthermore, children with suspected disabilities could be removed from regular classrooms or schools without informing parents or obtaining their permission. The LRE requirements of IDEA address the needless and unilateral segregation of children with disabilities.

Box 1.2
_____

A measure of the success of the LRE policies is that today over 96% of all students with disabilities are educated in regular schools. Fewer than 35,000 attend state residential schools, such as those for the deaf and blind. Over half of all students with disabilities spend 80% or more of their school day in regular class. Another 30% spend about 40% of their day in regular class. Only about a fifth of all special education students are educated in separate classes and another 4% are educated in separate schools or facilities. Most policymakers believe that we can still improve on the numbers of children educated at least part-time in general education classrooms.

_____

Source: U.S. Department of Education (2001).

Terms associated with LRE have included *mainstreaming, reverse mainstreaming, integration,* and *inclusion.* Some of the terms reflect different conceptions of LRE. The first three terms often are interpreted to mean that special education is provided outside of the general classroom or school and that individual students move back into general education after they meet certain criteria. Inclusive classrooms begin with the assumption that every student belongs to a general education classroom and is educated within that classroom with same-age peers. Special education and related services are provided in flexible arrangements to support access to the general education curriculum.

> For more information about training programs and other supports for paraeducators, see U.S. Office of Special Education Programs (2003) and Wallace, Pickett, and Liken (2002).

Today, inclusion is the generally accepted goal for educating students with disabilities in regular schools and classrooms. However, in school districts all over the United States, we find students with disabilities being educated in separate settings. Some parents and professionals remain concerned about the level of support offered in general education classrooms.

Box 1.3   Paraeducators and LRE

Paraeducators or paraprofessionals are increasingly relied on to provide support to individual students with disabilities in inclusive classrooms. In fact, often the paraeducator is responsible for providing the instruction to an individual student. A recent national study (*www.spense.org*) reported that paraeducators typically spend about 90% of their time in instruction, including tutoring, implementing behavior plans, meeting with classroom teachers, and making ad hoc decisions about how to modify specific assignments.

The knowledge and training of these individuals is critical, as you will see in the next section when we talk about the importance of ensuring that every student with a disability receives access to the general education curriculum.

Little research has been conducted on the effectiveness of using paraeducators. Many parents and special educators are concerned about the level of training and the amount of responsibility these individuals are given. There are also concerns that a student may become too dependent on a paraeducator and not learn how to self-regulate his or her behavior or work independently.

Several research-based training programs and curricula for paraeducators have been developed. Many of these are implemented in community colleges, but some strategies and approaches are used in schools. Programs also include strategies for training special education teachers in techniques to supervise paraeducators, which is a very critical skill.

WHAT DO WE KNOW ABOUT INCLUSION?

The IEP team determines what constitutes LRE for an individual student. The team is to *first* develop goals and objectives and *then* determine which placement or combination of placements will result in a child's progress toward those outcomes. The IEP team must include general education teachers and emphasizes the need for collaborative decision making in determining goals as well as the supports needed to educate a student in a general education classroom.

Various courts have decided that LRE may be interpreted differently for different students, depending on their IEP goals. What is least restrictive for one child is restrictive for another. The courts have established tests to address issues related to LRE. Here are some examples of these judicial standards:

1. Can the educational services that make the segregated setting superior feasibly be provided in a nonsegregated setting? If so, the segregated placement is *inappropriate.*

2. Was the inclusive setting considered before other placements?

3. Will the student achieve educational benefit from being in the general education setting?

4. What are the educational benefits of the general education classroom with additional supports and services?

5. What are the nonacademic benefits of interaction with non-disabled students?

6. What effect does the student with a disability have on the teacher and other students?

The courts have tended to say that when there is no educational benefit in an inclusive education setting for a child, the school is not necessarily held responsible for educating a child in an inclusive setting. Also, students with disabilities are expected to conform to the educational practices of the school, and if they cannot, courts have upheld the right of the school to place the student in a separate setting.

Different age groups, types of placements, and categories of disability as well as research findings on the benefits of inclusion complicate legal interpretations. Summaries of the research on educating students with disabilities in general education classrooms suggest that students with disabilities develop better communication and social skills and behave better when they are educated in inclusive classes and schools.

Furthermore, no studies to date have shown that including students with disabilities has a negative impact on students without disabilities.

Research has identified factors that influence whether inclusion is successful in a school. These include level of schoolwide commitment to inclusion, principal support and leadership, teacher attitudes, parent and family support, collaborative planning and teaching, focusing on both social and instructional inclusion, and peer acceptance and support.

> To learn more about the research on inclusion see Moore (1998) and McGregor and Vogelsberg (1998).

While inclusion remains an important goal, recent changes to IDEA have also put a focus on providing access to the general education curriculum. This means that a student is not simply placed in general education, but that he or she must have access to the curriculum in that classroom and progress in that curriculum. The central challenge for principals is how to bring together the requirements to provide an appropriate education within the most inclusive setting that will lead to higher levels of achievement for every student.

In the next section, we address this challenge as we discuss the basics of a new and evolving special education. This concept of special education is grounded more in producing better educational outcomes and accountability and less in legal procedures.

Least restrictive

response to intervention

disproportionate behavior

General Curriculum
in IEP
p.23

Designing Special Education for the 21st Century

Key Ideas for Section II

➢ Special education is evolving from a separate and parallel program within a school to a flexible set of resources and services that support students with disabilities' access to the general education curriculum.

➢ Principals and teachers must understand the difference between accommodations and modifications and the implications of each.

➢ A student with a disability is entitled to have accommodations on assessments, but not every student with a disability may need an assessment accommodation.

INTERPRETING ASSESSMENT RESULTS FOR STUDENTS WITH DISABILITIES

Now that we've discussed the basic structure of special education policy, we will turn to the features of high-quality special education programs. Creating a quality special education program requires that a principal know much more than the basic legal policies and procedures we discussed in the previous section.

A high-quality special education program has four features:

1. Students with disabilities have meaningful *access to the general education curriculum.*

2. Students with disabilities are fully included in all *assessment and accountability* systems.

3. Classroom and school environments *promote positive behavior* among all students

4. There is *strong parent and family communication.*

ACCESS TO THE GENERAL EDUCATION CURRICULUM

In 1997, several important changes were made to the IDEA to better align special education practices with the broader standards-driven reforms in general education. Chief among these changes were new provisions that require students with disabilities to participate in state and district assessments with necessary accommodations and that their assessment results were reported. In addition, IDEA requires alternate assessments for those (small numbers of) students for whom the general assessment is not appropriate. Recent changes in other federal legislation (e.g., Title I) are even more stringent in the demand for greater accountability for students with disabilities. Issues related to participation in assessments are discussed later in this section. Before we discuss assessment, however, we need to focus on the underlying intent of the assessment requirements, that is, to ensure that students with disabilities have an opportunity to learn the critical information and skills in the general education curriculum. The most important new changes made to IDEA were those requiring the IEP team to specify how a student will access and then progress in the general education curriculum and participate in assessments.

> A comprehensive resource for how to modify instruction to provide access to the general education curriculum can be found in Nolet and McLaughlin (2000).

The requirements to provide access to the general education curriculum pertain regardless of the setting in which a child with a disability is educated or who (e.g., general or special education teacher) is responsible for providing the student's education.

Box 2.1   Linking an IEP to Standards and Assessments

IEPs must include the following:

- A statement of the child's present levels of educational performance, including how the child's disability affects his or her involvement and progress in the general curriculum
- Measurable goals that meet the child's needs that result from his or her disability and allow the child to be involved in and progress in the general curriculum
- A statement of the special education and related services, supplementary aids and services, or program modifications that are to be provided to the child including a description of any modifications or supports that are necessary for the child to be involved and progress in the general curriculum, participate in extracurricular or other nonacademic activities, and be educated and participate in activities with other children with and without disabilities
- A statement of any individual modifications in the administration of state or district assessments of student achievement that are needed for the child to participate in the assessment; if the IEP team determines that the child will not participate in the assessment, the IEP must include a statement that tells why that assessment is not appropriate along with a description of how the child's achievement will be measured (e.g., alternate assessment)

We have found that many teachers and administrators are asking what it means to provide access to the general education curriculum. For many of these educators, the emphasis on providing access to the general education curriculum is a major challenge. They ask how students who are receiving special education because they have failed to make progress in some or all of the general curriculum can be expected to be put back into that same curriculum. Some educators view this requirement as synonymous with *inclusion*, meaning you have access if you are present *in* a general education classroom. However, accessing the general education curriculum is more complex than simply being placed in a general education classroom and will require new ways of thinking about the role of special education and how general education teachers think about instruction.

Creating a New Model for Special Education

There is a need to ensure that a student with a disability accesses the general education curriculum and that the student's IEP directly references the curriculum. In turn, the curriculum should be aligned with a state's content and performance standards. This is a new way of thinking about special education. The traditional model of special education viewed students with disabilities in relative isolation from general education. That is, a child was assessed; his or her learning strengths and deficits were identified; and individual goals, objectives, and strategies were devised to meet the deficits. Evaluations of whether a student met his or her IEP goals frequently were conducted in isolation from the general education curriculum and assessments. The IEP goals focused on short-term and discrete skill deficits and IEPs often were a collection of isolated skill objectives that led to isolated instruction. A student's program may have been individualized, but it could also be separated from the larger scope and sequence of the curriculum. Sometimes an IEP defined *the* curriculum for a student, instead of a tool for defining how to implement the general education curriculum.

The new model of special education, illustrated in Figure 2.1, is one in which special education is defined as a set of services and supports that are designed for an individual student to help him or her access and progress in the general education curriculum. In this model, special education students are represented within the rectangle. In some instances there may not be a marked difference between a general education student and a student receiving special education. However, the latter are entitled to have an individually tailored education plan. So let's think about how that plan should be developed.

Every student's IEP should be based on an assessment that indicates where he or she is situated in the scope and sequence of the general education curriculum. That is, we need to know what skills, concepts, and constructs the student has mastered. We also need to know what accommodations or modifications are needed to help a student progress or learn the curriculum, including specific instructional strategies, technologies, or other supports, and how the student's progress will be monitored. Special education can supplement the general education curriculum by

Figure 2.1   A New Model of Special Education

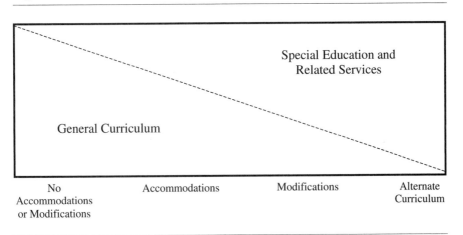

Source: Adapted from Nolet and McLaughlin (2000).

providing instruction in specific skill areas not addressed in the general education curriculum, such as social and behavioral skills or other more functional living skills. Decisions about an IEP are individualized, but they start from an understanding of the expectations of the general education curriculum and what is required to help the student access that curriculum.

Access to the Curriculum on a Continuum

Using Figure 2.1 as a guide, IEP planning for each child begins with the assumption that the student will be taught the subject matter defined by the general education curriculum *regardless of the setting or environment in which the student is being educated.* For some students, such as those receiving only speech and language services, no changes may be necessary to the content or the instruction that is provided within the general curriculum. The indicator arrow on Figure 2.2a shows that almost all of the instruction these students receive is in the general curriculum.

The next level of the access continuum assumes that instructional *accommodations* will be made, but that the student, like his or her peers in the classroom, will be expected to learn all of the curriculum content. That is, neither content nor performance standards are changed. As Figure 2.2b illustrates, a greater portion of the student's educational program involves special education and related services.

Figure 2.2   A New Model of Special Education: Changes in the Educational
Program

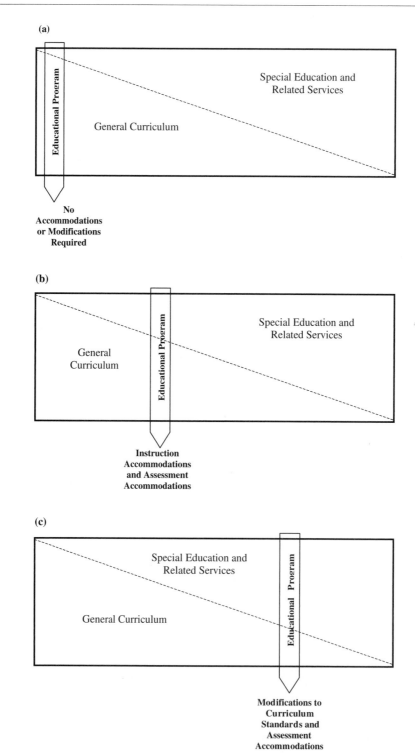

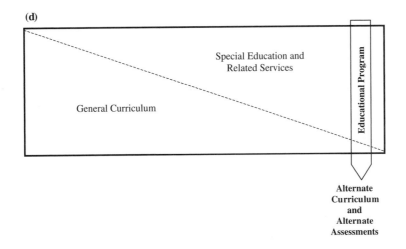

(d)

General Curriculum

Special Education and Related Services

Educational Program

Alternate Curriculum and Alternate Assessments

Understanding Accommodations

An accommodation does not change the content of instruction or the performance expectations. The student is expected to learn substantially the same information as the rest of the class and work toward the same content and performance standards as do the other students. Equally important is that the student is expected to *demonstrate* what he or she knows on the same assessments.

Accommodations *can* involve changes to the sequence in which material is presented or the timelines on which a student is expected to learn curriculum information: for example, allowing a student more time to complete an assignment or test, allocating more time for a student to complete a reading assignment, or changing a student's setting to a more quiet place. Often, accommodations involve use of certain technology, ranging from simple (e.g., pencil grips or large print books) to more complex (e.g., calculators, spell checkers, personal digital assistants, and laptop computers).

Accommodations also can involve changes to the type of instruction a student receives. For example, a student might be provided additional opportunities to practice or apply specific skills or concepts using a variety of materials or situations. An accommodation might entail providing direct instruction in a specific area when the general curriculum program is designed to be more student directed. Among the most powerful instructional accommodations a teacher can provide is increasing the time *allocated* to instruction in a particular content area.

One of the crucial roles the principal plays when an IEP team is considering accommodations is to help all members of the IEP team understand that an accommodation does not alter major learning outcomes expected of the instruction. The principal also can ensure that the IEP team includes a teacher or other member with a deep understanding of the curricular content domain that a student with a disability is expected to learn.

Modifications

Curricular *modifications* begin to change the expectations regarding what content a student learns as well as the expectations for learner achievement and outcomes. As Figure 2.2c illustrates, when modifications are made, a considerable portion of the student's program involves specially designed instruction. When a modification is made, a student's instructional program focuses on the same general subject matter and essential curricular goals as the general curriculum. However, there may be substantial adjustments to some or all of the performance expectations, the topics covered, the instructional sequences or timelines, or the instructional strategies employed. Modifications often involve use of different curriculum materials, such as providing lower-level reading material such as textbooks that are below the grade level of the class.

Modifications must be made with caution. They often reduce a student's opportunity to learn the critical knowledge, skills, and concepts in certain subject matter which, in turn, will affect his or her future ability to learn more difficult content. The effect of modifications can be to "dumb down" the curriculum to such an extent that the student no longer has access to the same curriculum as the rest of the class. For example, off-grade-level texts may reduce demands for reading and language skills, but they very likely present very different concepts, vocabulary, and other key skills. Remember, the cognitive complexity of the information contained in the curriculum increases along with the reading and language complexity of the texts.

The possible implications of modifying the curriculum are significant if they place the student at a disadvantage on assessments. Curricular modifications have both long- and short-term implications and need to be carefully designed by the IEP team.

Finally, a totally individualized set of content goals may be defined for a few students. As Figure 2.2d shows, when a student is receiving instruction in an *alternate or extensively individualized curriculum,* almost the entire educational program involves special education and related services.

Remember, fewer than 1% of students in schools would be expected to need an alternate curriculum. These are students whose disabilities are so complex as to require programs of high intensity or duration. Programs at this end of the curriculum often involve functional skills associated with daily living, mobility, and communication. The curriculum may be aligned with the standards of the general education curriculum, but a very different set of performance outcomes likely will be established and measured, using alternate assessments.

Box 2.2   Examples of Accommodations and Modifications

Accommodations do not change the content or performance expectations. They may change the sequence in which information is presented or they may entail differentiated instruction. Examples can include

- Sign language
- Braille materials
- Recorded books
- Adaptive technology
- Content enhancements such as advance organizers and study guides
- Scribes or tape recorders instead of pencil and paper
- Additional opportunities for practice
- Additional examples or applications of skills or concepts

Modifications may involve changes to performance expectations, topics taught, curriculum sequences, or the type of instruction delivered. They do not change curriculum standards toward which a student works. Examples can include

- Out-of-level texts
- Materials adjusted for reading level
- Fewer pages in a reading assignment
- Fewer problems in a homework assignment
- Fewer steps in a problem-solving activity
- Alternative expectations in a group assignment
- Fewer or simpler goals or objectives
- Skills instruction instead of content instruction

A Decision-Making Process for Developing IEPs

As a principal, you might ask, "Why do I have to understand all of this information about IEP development?" There are three reasons:

1. As the instructional leader of a school you need to understand the critical role of the IEP in the instruction of students with disabilities.

2. You are responsible for ensuring that these students benefit from having high expectations and a high-quality curriculum.

3. You are accountable for improving the performance of all students in your building.

By now you know that the IEP is the centerpiece of planning a student's special education services or supports. The IEP should be more than simply a legal document that lists goals and objectives and services. It should reflect the decisions of a team regarding how special education will support access to the curriculum as well as provide instruction on other areas relevant to a child's long-term educational goals (see Figure 2.3). A principal has a key role in helping make this decision process a success.

There are three basic phases in IEP planning:

Phase 1: Identify the critical, enduring knowledge associated with the general curriculum that all students will learn (usually based on state and district standards).

Phase 2: Analyze the key knowledge and skills that a competent individual uses to perform tasks associated with that knowledge. This step is generally analogous to the process of task analysis familiar to many special educators. However, the work we are talking about here is *not* the same as the highly detailed analysis that IEP teams often conduct and that frequently results in irrelevant goals and objectives focused on small subcomponents of basic skills.

Phase 3: Analyze the individual child's use of key learning processes and strategies.

Goal Setting

In addition to general curricular goals, IEPs must include any additional skills and knowledge areas beyond the general curriculum to be addressed through special education or related services. These goals will also need to be specified. Important questions for setting IEP goals include those shown in Box 2.4.

Considerations when modifying the general education curriculum are listed in Box 2.5.

You should now see that access to the general education curriculum represents a complex set of decisions based on information about how well a student is currently performing in the general education curriculum as well as knowledge of the expectations for that student's performance in future years. In other words, what does the student need to know and be able to do by the end of elementary and middle school or by the time he or she is a young adult? Also required is a discussion of the implications of

Figure 2.3   An IEP Decision-Making Process

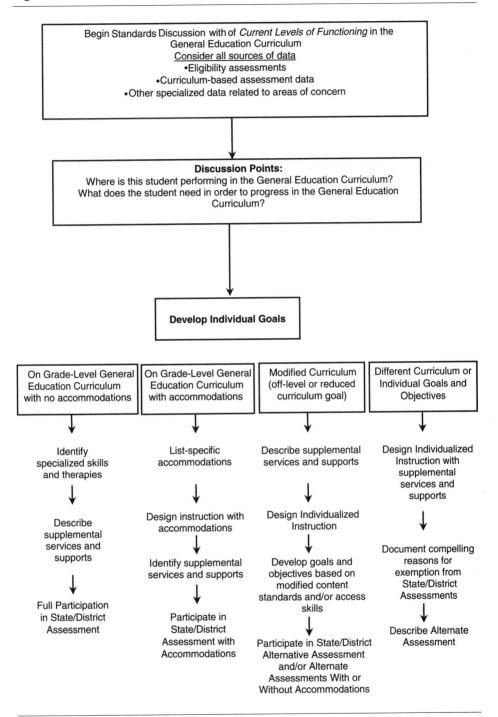

Source: Adapted from Nolet and McLaughlin (2000).

modifying or changing the curriculum. Remember, test results will not improve if students with disabilities do not have an opportunity to learn the material that is being assessed.

Box 2.3

Some Questions That Can Help Guide the IEP Planning Process Include

1. What will typical students be expected to do (math, science, reading, PE, and so on) during this time frame addressed by the IEP (this grading period, semester, year)?

   Usually you will want goals and objectives and standards to define the student performances expected. Examples include being able to read specific text independently and answer questions, being able to accurately estimate size and measurement in a variety of daily situations, and being able to write a minimum of four paragraphs that logically develop an idea while conforming to rules of grammar and punctuation.

2. How is the target student currently performing in these areas?

   Look at classroom evidence regarding the key areas as well as input from parents, teachers, and other team members. The idea is to decide where the student falls on a continuum of competence on the standards or broad curriculum goals as well as skills they use for learning.

3. In what ways are the student's disabilities impacting the performance?

   In addition to specific skill deficits such as in reading or math, educational assessments should consider such things as attention or focus, memory, organizational skills, and communication as well as other learning processes.

4. What accommodations and supports will the student need to offset the impact of the disability?

   For example, will they need memory aids, communication assistance, specific organizational strategies, more intensive instruction in certain areas, and so forth.

Box 2.4

- What do we expect the student to be able to do at the end of this instructional year?
  The list of targets encompasses general curriculum as well as specialized knowledge and skill areas.

- Do we expect the student to be able to demonstrate the same performances and outcomes in the subject matter as the typical student?
  Will the student need accommodations? If so, which ones? Which alternative methods will the student receive? Instruction may be provided in addition to that delivered to others. For example, a student may receive reading instruction through a more explicit approach than other students in the class. There may also be additional opportunities for reteaching using more representations and for practice.

Box 2.5

- Will we teach the same content but lower the performance expectation?
  Here the decision is to provide an opportunity for the student to be exposed to all of the same knowledge and instruction that is provided to the typical student, but to reduce the expectations of what the student will have to demonstrate. This decision is very much related to teaching less content but assumes that the student should receive instruction in all of what is taught, but he or she will only be expected to learn less.

- Will we teach less content?
  There are a variety of ways to make this modification: the student learns fewer objectives or curricular benchmarks, the student completes shorter units or parts of a unit, the student reads fewer pages or paragraphs, or the student participates in shorter lessons or parts of lessons.

- Will we set alternative goals?
  As we have previously noted, every student could have some IEP goals that reflect very specific skills or knowledge that is required to address the impacts of the disability. However, with respect to alternative curriculum goals, we refer to those few students who are working toward an individualized set of instructional goals or objectives, either within the same subject matter areas as their peers or in different areas.

Box 2.6   A Real-Life Example of How Special and General Education Teachers Provide Access

In Westlake School District (not its real name), special and general education teachers have a history of collaborative planning and teaching. Originally, this was done to promote inclusion or the education of students with disabilities in general education classrooms. The district had provided professional development to both general and special education teachers in coteaching models and collaborative consultation. But, as the district implemented new content standards and tough new local and state assessments, the focus moved to ensuring that all students accessed the curricular standards. They were not just in the general education classrooms; they were learning core and essential knowledge and skills. A typical scenario in one of the district's middle schools follows:

Ms. Austin, a special educator, is assigned to the sixth grade team. She meets regularly with the team to discuss issues related to the curriculum and other team issues. However, Ms. Austin also meets individually with each of the content teachers in the team to discuss in-depth the units of instruction that will be covered during a grading period. Ms. Austin's conversations go something like this: "Basically, we talk about what they are planning to cover in the next grading period. In particular, we review the key concepts and the standards that will be addressed. The [content] teacher discusses the essential knowledge or skills that he or she wants every kid to really learn. I know that my job is to help the students with IEPs and 504 plans learn that. I focus my instruction and support on those areas. . . . We both agree that not everything that goes on in the class is of equal value. We need to focus our time and the kids' efforts on the standards that matter."

In one of the district's elementary schools, the special education teachers talk about loading up on planning time with the general education teachers at the beginning of the year and before each marking period. The principal finds time, using subs and creative scheduling, to allow for the special and general education teacher to meet to discuss the critical curriculum goals that should be the focus of the intensive support and instruction. Planning and communication during the grading period happens "on the fly" or in class, unless there is a specific problem. "We don't need regularly scheduled time to meet since we have already understood what each of us is to be focusing on. We can debrief and keep on track on an ongoing basis."

ASSESSMENT AND ACCOUNTABILITY

As we noted earlier, assessment and accountability for results are the mainstays of current special and general education policies. For students with disabilities, this is a new arena and can be complex and poorly understood. Special educators have historically relied on the IEP as the chief accountability tool, but this is changing under the new Title I requirements of No Child Left Behind (NCLB) legislation and IDEA. The IEP has never been particularly effective as an accountability tool. First, it is a private document such that whether a student meets specific goals is known only within the team. Second, as an individual measure of a students' performance, research has demonstrated that it is easy to simply blame the student for failing to meet goals and to subsequently lower the standards. Only recently has special education been brought fully into the new accountability reforms. In 1997, the IDEA was amended to include several new provisions that call for students with disabilities to participate in state and local assessments.

Title I of NCLB further solidified these requirements by specifying that students with disabilities will be assessed and schools, local districts, and states will need to report their results separately and establish annual performance targets for this group of students.

Under the IDEA, Section 504, and the ADA, students with disabilities are entitled to receive accommodations if they require them. Earlier, we discussed the difference between an accommodation and a modification.

There are several important things that principals need to understand about including students with disabilities in their state and local assessments. These are

- Assessment accommodations
- Alternate assessments
- Reporting scores and adequate yearly progress (AYP)
- Legal issues

Assessment Accommodations

It is important to remember that an assessment accommodation is not intended to alter the construct that is being measured; it should only offset the impact of the disability. Most often assessment accommodations are used in combination, such as in allowing more time, having someone read the test to the student, and administering the assessment in a separate room.

Box 2.7

Under IDEA States Must

- Include students with disabilities in local and statewide assessments with accommodations where appropriate
- Report the performance of these students with the same frequency and in the same detail that they use to report nondisabled students' performance levels
- Develop alternate means of assessment for those students who are unable to participate in standard assessments and report the performance of these students.

Title I of NCLB Requires That

- Students with disabilities participate in all state assessments, with necessary accommodations
- Assessment results must be disaggregated and reported separately
- AYP must be calculated for each subgroup and based on the same proficiency goal
- Only a very small percentage (suggested at 1% of the student population) may be assessed using an alternate assessment
- Special education teachers must meet the highly qualified teacher standards
- All conditions applied to schools needing improvement must address students with disabilities in those schools

Box 2.8   Types of Assessment Accommodations

- *Setting.* Change the test location to allow a child to take the test in a small group or individually
- *Timing.* Allow extended time or take frequent test breaks
- *Scheduling.* Allow testing over several days or administer only during a specific time
- *Presentation.* Change format, use assistive device such as allowing a reader, provide computer assistance
- *Response.* Change how student responds—scribe, recorder, computer

Can a Student Have Any Type of Accommodation?

The IEP team is to decide which assessment accommodations a student with a disability requires. The accommodations should be provided in instruction as well as during the assessment. However, not every accommodation that an individual student needs in instruction is permissible with every test, nor is every test accommodation necessarily relevant to instruction. For example, in a high-stakes test, a student with a disability might take the assessment in a quiet room with extended time to minimize distractions. However, a simple spelling test or other class-room assessment might be given with the rest of the class if the teacher and student believe it will not interfere with performance.

Some accommodations invalidate an assessment. For example, having someone read a test that is assessing a students' ability to decode text clearly invalidates the construct (e.g., decoding print) that is being measured. Similarly, using a calculator on an assessment of mathematical computation invalidates that test. However, reading a test that measures how well a student comprehends text might not change the construct nor will a calculator necessarily invalidate a math reasoning test.

If a student requires an accommodation that is not permitted on the test, the student should receive the accommodation and should take the test. However, it is likely that the student's score is not included in a school's accountability index or school progress measure.

Do Accommodations Affect Student Test Scores?

This is perhaps the most controversial and most researched issue related to assessing students with disabilities. There has also been quite a bit of research about the topic, but there is yet to be a definite answer about the effects of accommodations.

We do know, for example, that the most common accommodation offered to students with disabilities is providing extended time. But, most often a student receives more than one accommodation on an assessment, such as having more time and taking the test in a small group or private setting. Some research conducted in very controlled studies suggests that effects of accommodations can be positive or negative depending on an individual student. This means that an accommodation that seems to improve one student's performance may actually detract from another student's. Other research has suggested that for some accommodations, such as extended time, many students with disabilities who receive this accommodation do not actually end up needing it because they can finish the test in the standard amount of time.

A good source for recent research related to assessment and accommodations and students with disabilities is the National Center on Educational Outcomes (www.education.umn.edu/nceo/). See Thurlow, Elliott, and Ysseldyke (1998).

These findings point to the need to be sure that a student receives accommodations during instruction that will also be provided on an assessment. Matching accommodations to a student's needs *in order to offset the impact of a disability* is the intent of the law as well as good education.

What Is an Alternate Assessment?

The IDEA requires that states develop alternate means for assessing those students who are unable to participate in standard assessments. The law does not specify what the alternate assessment should be, but the intent is to ensure that every student's performance and progress is accounted for. State education agencies have a variety of policies concerning what alternate assessments are permitted and which students should be assessed. The NCLB currently specifies that not more than 1% of the total school population may receive an alternate assessment. You should check with your local district special education administrator and your state department of education to determine the policies regarding alternate assessments in your state and district.

Am I Accountable for Alternate Assessments Results?

The short answer to this question is "yes." Both IDEA and NCLB require that the results of alternate assessments be reported and NCLB requires the results to be included in the AYP requirements. Currently, many states only report how many students with disabilities took an alternate assessment but do not report the results, or they report these assessment results only at the state level. Even when results of alternate assessments are available, they may not be reported at the school level due to the small numbers of students and the confidentiality concerns.

What Should I Look for in Score Reports?

In Section III we will discuss the importance of using data for school improvement as well as some of the challenges associated with obtaining data for students with disabilities. However, principals need to become much better users of performance data that have been disaggregated for students with disabilities. Specifically, principals need to track how many students with disabilities are taking state and local tests and the alternate assessments and understand why a student might be exempted. Principals should also know how many of which accommodations are being used and how many, if any, scores are not being reported or included in their school's AYP index due to nonstandard accommodations.

Principals should also be able to interpret whether individual students with disabilities as well as the group of these students are making progress. This can be a challenge if the assessments do not have enough items or opportunity to show small gains. If certain students are always scoring below the floor on an assessment and in those assessments in which a student must make a big jump in performance in order to move to the next score level, the school must have other assessments to indicate individual student and group progress. These assessments need to be aligned with the curriculum and the content of the state and local assessments.

Legal Considerations Related to Assessment

Several court cases have influenced considerations regarding a student's participation in general education assessments. These include the following:

The *Board of Education of the Hendrick Hudson School District v. Rowley* (1982) has application to the standards to which a student with a disability is to be held as well as the obligation of the school system to provide accommodations to support performance based on these standards. *Brookhart v. Illinois State Board of Education* (1983) concerned students with disabilities who did not pass their graduation tests and were denied high school diplomas. The court ruled that an inability to learn material cannot be overlooked in granting diplomas. However, the court also noted that Section 504 and special education law require that a test be valid and be suited for its intended purpose and appropriate for the group being tested. A leading court decision on test-based graduation requirements is *Debra P. v. Turlington* (1981). This decision concerned Black students who had attended illegally segregated schools in Florida and were failing the state competency exams. The courts ruled that the state could not withhold diplomas until the students had an opportunity to attend integrated schools and an opportunity to learn what was being assessed.

Recently, in *Rene v. Reed* (2001), a federal court of appeals upheld the right of Indiana to restrict the type of accommodations permitted on the high school exit examination if they would invalidate the results of the assessment. In Oregon, the state and advocates reached a settlement in a case alleging that the statewide assessment program discriminated against learning disabled students. A blue-ribbon panel was convened and made the following recommendations: increase the numbers of allowable accommodations, provided that they are used as part of the student's instruction and the state cannot prove that they will invalidate the score interpretation, and make available both alternate scoring procedures and alternate assessments to students with learning disabilities for any component of an assessment that is essential to receipt of a diploma.

A federal district court in *Chapman et al. v. California Department of Education* (2002) halted the administration of the California High School Exit Exam. The court determined that students with disabilities must be permitted to take the exam with any accommodation or modification

> For a more complete discussion of legal issues see Karger and Pullin (2002).

specified on their IEPs for testing or for general classroom instruction. Furthermore, if the IEP calls for an alternate assessment, one must be provided for the high school assessment as well.

PROMOTING POSITIVE BEHAVIOR OR HOW TO AVOID THE DISCIPLINE PROBLEM

Probably nothing creates as much anxiety, frustration, and overall confusion for principals as the procedures that apply to students who receive special education. It is as important that principals understand the origins of current legal requirements related to discipline and students with disabilities as it is to understand the requirements themselves.

However, even more important to the role of a school leader is to understand how to create a schoolwide system of positive behavioral supports for managing the array of disciplinary events that might be encountered in a school. We will begin with a brief overview of current legal procedures related to discipline and students who receive special education and how those procedures evolved. It will follow with a description of the concept of *positive behavioral supports,* or PBSs.

An Overview of Current Discipline Policies

The IDEA has required that certain procedures be followed for students with disabilities with respect to disciplinary actions that result in suspension or expulsion. These legal requirements have resulted in a dual discipline system in which the same infraction can result in one set of consequences for students without disabilities and one for students receiving special education. As this book goes to press the disciplinary procedures are being reconsidered. Changes are likely. However, below we provide an overview of current procedures that make sense and likely will remain in law.

The IEP and Discipline of Students With Disabilities

Much of the responsibility for anticipating and managing behavioral problems rests with the IEP team. If the team anticipates that behavior might be an issue for a student it should be able to analyze the causes and consequences of the behavior as well as develop specific intervention plans. Generally, there are two areas that must be addressed in developing the IEP:

A. In general, in developing each child's IEP, the IEP team shall consider
    1. The strengths of the child and the concerns of the parents for enhancing the education of their child
    2. The results of the initial evaluation or most recent evaluation of the child

B. Special factors should be considered
    1. In the case of a child whose behavior impedes his or her learning or that of others
    2. The IEP team shall consider, when appropriate, strategies including positive behavioral interventions and supports that address that behavior (20 USC 1414(d)(3).

The IEP team should be able to conduct *functional behavioral assessments* (FBAs) as part of the evaluation of a child and design and implement *behavioral intervention plans* (BIPs). Discipline procedures concerning removal of a student with a disability are complex and principals should be familiar with their state and district procedures regarding placement in alternative educational settings, determining if the behavior is a manifestation of the students' disability, and what to do if parents appeal. Also, as noted, these procedures may likely change in coming years.

Why IDEA Requires Different Disciplinary Procedures

There are two major provisions of IDEA that support different disciplinary procedures. The first is the primary legal entitlement of IDEA to a free appropriate public education (FAPE). The entitlement to FAPE is not conditional. It applies to any student who receives special education regardless of his or her characteristics or situation. Thus the fact that a student may have engaged in a behavior that the school believes should result in a suspension or expulsion does not nullify that student's entitlement to FAPE. Students with disabilities must still receive the special education and related services to which they are entitled.

The entitlement to be educated in the least restrictive environment requires that the IEP team determine what constitutes the LRE for any given student and requires the parent's or parents' agreement to that placement. The IDEA requires that parents be notified in writing of any proposed changes in the educational placement of their child with a disability. If parents object to the change, the law requires the student with an IEP to "stay put" until a full review has been completed.

These basic entitlements and protections are offered to every student with an IEP and have been interpreted through specific court cases to apply to certain disciplinary measures, specifically suspension and expulsion, that are considered changes in placement. The 1988 U.S. Supreme Court decision *Honig v. Doe* (484 S.Ct. 305) set down many of the legal standards that schools must follow in cases in which students with disabilities are considered for suspension or expulsion. The case involved two emotionally disturbed children in California who were given 5-day suspensions from school for acts that included destroying school property and assaulting other students. The suspensions were continued indefinitely while expulsion proceedings were considered. The students sued, citing the extended suspensions as violation of the stay-put provision.

The Supreme Court declared that the purpose of the stay-put provision was to prevent schools from changing a student's educational placement over his or her parents' objection. While the IDEA currently provides for interim placements of students if parents and school officials agree on one, no emergency exception for dangerous students is included. However, where a student with a disability poses an immediate threat to the safety of others, school officials may temporarily suspend him or her for up to 10 school days without constituting a change in placement.

The current discipline procedures required by IDEA are consequences of previous discriminatory treatment of children with disabilities. At the same time, both general and special educators agree that the procedures can be cumbersome and can create a great deal of tension between special and general education in the schools. Furthermore, there is no evidence that the procedures alone have fixed a student's particular behavioral problems. They have, however, prevented students with disabilities from being denied education and treatment.

Creating Positive Behavioral Supports

In recent years, the focus has shifted from a reactive response to behavior problems among students with disabilities to one that focuses on prevention. This has resulted in a research-validated approach to behavior called positive behavioral supports (PBSs).

What Is PBS?

The fundamentals of PBS are based on a three-level conceptual model of behavioral problems in schools developed by researchers at the University of Oregon. The key features of PBS include an emphasis on prevention, active instruction aimed at improving social behaviors, using data to make decisions about individual students and program effects, using research validated strategies, and involving entire systems within and outside the school. The model has been thoroughly tested in schools across the United States.

> For more in-depth information, visit the American Institutes for Research Web site at www.air.org and the Research and Training Center on Family Support and Children's Mental Health Web site at www.rtc.pdx.edu

The three parts of the model include (1) prevention strategies designed to reduce or eliminate new problems as well as the serious events among a small number of students, (2) specific attention to teaching appropriate behavioral and social skills, and (3) carefully analyzing individual students' behaviors and monitoring overall progress.

1. Emphasis on prevention—There are three levels of prevention in the PBS framework (see Figure 2.4).

   - *Primary prevention:* The goal here is to decrease the number of new behavioral problems or disciplinary events in the school through use of schoolwide and classwide behavior management strategies and better instructional practices.

   - *Secondary prevention:* The goal is to reduce the numbers of students who have demonstrated some problems that put them at risk of becoming a behavior problem. Interventions are usually more specialized and focus on small groups of students. They can include counseling, conflict resolution strategies, social skills training, anger management, and similar specialized programs. In addition, many of the students who need secondary prevention strategies are at risk of school failure and may need intensive academic support.

   - *Tertiary prevention:* This level of intervention is highly specialized and is targeted toward reducing the number, frequency, and severity of behavioral incidents among a small number of students with serious behavior and emotional difficulties. Interventions are almost always designed by a team, including behavioral specialists, and are highly tailored to the individual. These students typically have IEPs; however, it is possible that

Figure 2.4   The Levels of Prevention

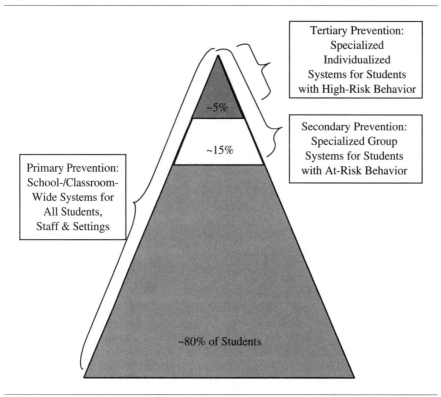

Source: From "Introduction to the special series on positive behavior supports in school" by G. Sugai and R. H. Horner (2002). *Journal of Emotional and Behavioral Disorders, 10,* 130–135. © 2002 by PRO-ED, Inc. Reprinted with permission.

students may have serious emotional or behavioral problems without having an adverse impact on their academic achievement and thus not be eligible to receive special education.

2. Improving social behaviors—Attempts to manage or correct problem behavior are more effective when they are accompanied by a systematic approach that supports positive behaviors. Research with PBS has demonstrated that this approach includes the following:

   • Promoting academic success and a feeling of efficacy among students and teachers; in other words, students believe that they can achieve and learn and teachers believe that they are effective in managing their classrooms and helping children learn

   • Promoting consistent classroom and school routines and expectations about behavior and civility

- Making clear to students what exactly is expected in various situations and providing opportunities to practice and demonstrate to students the specific social expectations

3. Using data to make decisions—In the area of behavior, functional behavioral assessments are central to developing behavioral interventions at the secondary and tertiary levels. An FBA is a team process that involves

- Collecting specific information about a student's behavior, what appeared to prompt the behavior, and the consequences

- Developing hypotheses about what might be causing certain behaviors or maintaining the behaviors

- Developing individualized behavioral intervention plans that use the assessment information to develop strategies that focus on the social and personal strengths of the student (such as family or peer networks, abilities, or interests) and at the same time make the problem behavior ineffective or inefficient (in other words, eliminate the payoff to the student or make the behavior irrelevant)

- Understanding that BIPs will only be effective if they are developed in a collaborative structure so that all individuals—specialists, teachers, the principal, parents, and the student—clearly understand what the interventions are and accept responsibility for ensuring that the specific strategies are implemented

> Not sure if your staff knows how to conduct *functional behavioral assessments?* See *Teaching Exceptional Children 35*(5), May/June 2003, a publication of the Council for Exceptional Children.

- Monitoring the effects of the intervention; too often a BIP is implemented and no one takes responsibility for monitoring if the strategies are being implemented as intended or if the student's behavior improves

Building Strong Parent and Family Connections

Parents and families have always been critical to achieving the goals of IDEA just as parents and families are important to schooling in general. Indeed, Standard 4 of the ISLLC states, "A school administrator is an educational leader who promotes the success of all students by collaborating with families and community members, responding to diverse community interests and needs, and mobilizing community resources."

Box 2.9

A recent 2-year study was conducted by Nelson, Martella, and Marchand-Martella (2002) in seven elementary schools in which positive behavior support systems were implemented. The seven study schools were then compared to 28 other elementary schools in the district in a number of areas. Each school went through the following phases:

- School faculty identified specific problems and gaps in programs and services
- A leadership team was created to guide the process
- Schoolwide practices were assessed and interventions designed and approved by faculty consensus that addressed schoolwide organizational practices, schoolwide classroom-management practices, and individualized behavioral intervention plans
- Progress was monitored through use of office referrals and other discipline data, teacher surveys, and interviews.

A schoolwide assessment addressed issues related to space and scheduling.

- Space issues that contributed to behavior problems included playground areas that were out of view and not supervised where prohibited activities, including bullying, would occur; isolated spots in hallways where certain students could gravitate outside of supervision; and poor bus-loading routines and areas that contribute to confusion and too many students congregated in one place.
- Scheduling issues including decreasing wait time and travel time between classrooms, lunch, recess, and so forth; clearly marking transition zones between a controlled area and common areas, letting students know where they were in the school and what was expected in each zone; and minimizing large groups of students, particularly cross-grades, in any contained part of the building or playground.

Behavioral expectations for all students were defined by teachers through a consensus-building process. Teachers first established expectations for the common areas or routines, lunch, arrival, and departure because the majority of problems occurred during these times.

- Teachers broke the expectations into specific teachable behaviors, not just rules on a piece of poster board.
- Students were taught the expectations through a three-phase process: first they were highly supervised and given a lot of praise and corrective feedback for the first several weeks of school, then they were given periodic structured practice or review sessions, and, finally, they had booster sessions as needed.
- Teachers agreed on common supervision strategies and a consistent approach. Teachers understood which behaviors warranted an office referral. They also learned a common set of interventions to problem behaviors that they were to implement in their classrooms or common areas.
- A one-to-one reading program was established along with a conflict resolution program.
- A family intervention specialist was brought in to develop a voluntary video-based program for families of students with the highest rate of discipline problems.
- Teams developed individualized behavioral intervention plans for those students with the most serious or frequent behavioral problems.

The seven schools significantly reduced administrative disciplinary actions; increased academic achievement scores in reading, language arts, spelling, science, and social studies; and increased social competence and academic scores among students with the most challenging behaviors. In addition, teachers reported that they were highly satisfied with the process and outcomes.

In special education, the role of parents has been strengthened so that they may better participate in the decisions regarding their child. Parents are entitled to provide information about their child during the child's initial evaluation to determine eligibility for special education. They are also entitled to be part of the group that makes the decision regarding their child's eligibility. Parents have the opportunity to examine *all* records pertaining to their child, not just education records, and must provide informed consent for their child to be reevaluated after placement in special education. Parents are to be full partners in developing their child's IEP and consenting to placements and educational goals and objectives.

Recent changes within IDEA also encourage the use of strategies for avoiding and resolving disputes between parents and schools. Parents must now notify the state or local education agency before requesting a due process hearing. This allows the public agencies to be informed and, presumably, to take actions that may resolve a problem without the formality and expense of a due-process procedure.

What Is Parent Involvement?

Creating a collaborative relationship between parents of children with disabilities and educators is a major goal shared by parent advocates, administrators, and policymakers. A key factor in creating good partnerships with parents is understanding what constitutes *effective* parent involvement.

Principals often view parent involvement in terms of volunteering in the school and directly supporting or reinforcing school requirements with their child. Principals are urged to offer a variety of opportunities for parents to become involved in their schools, and teachers and principals would like to see parents take an active role in monitoring homework and supporting discipline decisions. The participation of parents of special education students involves all of the above and more. Good collaboration requires an understanding regarding the needs of many of those parents.

Box 2.10   Voices of Real Parents

"I really don't talk much at my son's IEP meetings because I am trying so hard not to cry. Even though he's 12, every time I go to the IEP it just brings up again all the reality about his disability."

"I just wish the school would at least act like they liked my child and when my husband and I come in they would treat us more informally. They always act so formal and then we go into a room with all of these people sitting there who have been talking about our child . . . and us."

"We need respect. . . . We need to feel that our contribution is valued. We need to participate, not merely be involved. It is, after all, the parent who knew the child first and who knows the child best. Our relationship with our sons and daughters is personal and spans a lifetime."

What might have made a difference for these parents? What constitutes meaningful collaboration and participation for them? What are the strategies for promoting effective collaboration and communication between parents and families of students with disabilities and the school?

Taking the Perspective of the Parent of a Child With a Disability

Principals are expected to work with all parents and their school community. It is particularly important that principals communicate, collaborate with, and involve parents in the education of their child with a disability. In turn, principals should expect that parents of children with disabilities be partners with the school and help resolve any issues that might arise. Principals may believe that they are doing everything possible to collaborate with the parents of children with disabilities. Principals may honestly believe they are cooperating and communicating. From the parents' perspective, the interactions can be frustrating, often because they do not feel that the school understands their unique concerns about their child's disability.

To be able to work effectively with parents of students with disabilities a principal must understand and respect the perspective of those parents. Parents of children with disabilities, like all other parents, want a good education for their child, but they can also have additional anxieties about their child, including safety, peer acceptance, teasing or bullying, and fears that they are not learning or making enough progress.

Box 2.11

According to Patricia Smith, a parent of an adult with disabilities and long-time parent educator and advocate, "When parents learn about any difficulty or problem in their child's development, this information comes as a tremendous blow."

Parents experience intense emotions about their child's disability, regardless of how severe the disability may be or at what point it is diagnosed. For parents of a child who has a severe disability that might be diagnosed at birth or in the early years these emotions can be denial and anger accompanied by fear of what the future brings. Parents whose children are diagnosed later, usually after some years of failure and problems in the school, often are frustrated and tired from the repeated calls from schools, conferences, and attempts to "fix" their child's problem. Many parents of children with disabilities feel guilty and have a great deal of anxiety about what that future holds for their child. Sometimes the emotional and physical weariness associated with parenting a child with a disability can immobilize the parent. They may just give up so that the school may see a parent who is not involved or doesn't care instead of a parent who needs support or direction. For other parents the anxieties about their child lead them to be even more vigilant of the school and to question decisions made by the school.

Parents of children with disabilities can often feel powerless in the education process of their child. Despite the rights of parents of children with disabilities to be involved in all phases of their child's educational program, the parents often do not feel competent to make critical decisions. They must rely on experts and professionals to explain to them what their child needs. This requires a great deal of trust, and often the professionals are strangers to the parents or someone they do not know well. Yet, trust is the foundation of effective parent collaboration and involvement.

Involve Parents of Children With Disabilities in Schoolwide Activities

The IDEA makes it clear that parents of children with disabilities are to be involved in specific policymaking bodies. An important way to involve parents of children with disabilities is in the school improvement planning process. Asking these parents to review data concerning special education students and to be part of a process of developing school goals and activities, including those that may pertain specifically to children with disabilities, is important for many reasons. First, it engages these parents in the school community. Sometimes the parents of children with disabilities do not feel connected to a school. If this is not the home school of the child and the family is not part of the neighborhood, there can be a greater distance between the school and the parents. Second, it is important for all parents to see the big picture in terms of what the school as a whole is moving toward as well as how special education fits within the overall program. Many parents, and perhaps more parents of children with disabilities, can develop tunnel vision when it comes to their child's needs. It is important for every parent to understand their child's needs within the context of the larger school. But often parents of children with disabilities feel that they have been shut out of decision making in schools. Make sure that when you do involve parents in schoolwide plans you are hearing the voices of all the parents, including parents of children with various disabilities.

Don't Be Afraid to Give Parents Information

A good relationship with parents depends on open communication and parents having access to the teacher, a counselor, a school psychologist, or the principal. Principals need to ensure that parents have opportunities to communicate about their child. Developing an open and trusting relationship with *one person,* typically a special education teacher, is a key to good parental cooperation.

Parents of children with disabilities often need more information regarding the expectations of the school. For example, parents may need more information about test scores, grades, and other assessments to help them understand how their child is really progressing.

A frequent comment made by parents concerning grading is, "I know that my child is not doing grade-level work, but what I really want to know is, are they improving in reading or math? What can we expect by next year? Do we need to do something different?"

Real participation can only occur when you have informed parents. Don't be afraid of giving information to parents of children with disabilities. Open communication is part of building trust. Make certain that they have information about their rights (most school districts have information about parent's rights under special education law) and give them other information or resources. Perhaps your special education director can provide some materials or you can direct a parent to one of the many Web sites that have excellent information. If there is something you don't know, say so and ask the parent for information. The Web site www.nichcy.org is a particularly good resource for materials to help you inform and involve parents in your school.

Encourage all staff to use layperson language and make it a practice to do a language check in IEP or other meetings with the parents. Just pause and ask if anyone has any questions about a word or term that has been used.

Principals need to be well informed about who the students with disabilities are in their school and to be sensitive to the various stresses of parenting a child with a disability. Principals must assume leadership for ensuring parental involvement, including assessing the degree to which parents are participating in the education of their child and how satisfied they are with the opportunities for involvement. The goal for principals should be to create a partnership with parents, based on mutual respect and understanding. This will require open communication, respect, and time as well as principals who are supportive and proactive.

SUMMARY

In this section we have discussed the following key features of good special education in a school: (1) all students with disabilities must have access to the general education curriculum and progress in that curriculum, (2) all students with disabilities must participate in state and local assessments and schools must be accountable for improving their performance, (3) schools should adopt a schoolwide approach to social and behavioral supports that prevents problems as well as reduces the frequency and severity of problems among certain students, and (4) schools must have open parent communication and meaningful parent engagement. Effective special education is not that different from effective education.

Several themes are apparent throughout our discussion of the above features. These include references to collaboration and team decision making and careful assessment and monitoring of practices and student progress. In addition, we have been careful to only suggest practices for which there is sufficient evidence or research to suggest that they are valid. In Section III we turn to the three themes or processes that are necessary to create the effective special education practices we have discussed.

Resources for Creating a Quality Special Education Program in Your School

Key Ideas for Section III

➤ High-quality special education programs must be built around instructional practices that have a proven track record and have been validated by sound research.
➤ Principals should use a systematic process for making data-based decisions and model and promote data-based decision making throughout the school.
➤ Quality special education requires a collaborative culture throughout the entire school.

ADOPT PROVEN INSTRUCTIONAL PRACTICES

Among the new responsibilities of school leaders is ensuring that decisions to implement specific instructional models or curricular approaches are based on research, the expertise of teachers, and the recommendations of professional organizations. A principal must help all staff in the school investigate the instructional practices they choose and select only those that have a proven record of success.

On a daily basis, principals are faced with a barrage of commercial advertisements touting everything from student fund-raising schemes to budget management software, reading curricula, professional development programs, and all types of technology. In addition, principals are often faced with opportunities to participate in model programs or to write grants for special programs. If you are a fan of the marketplace, you might welcome the availability of a wide variety of approaches and options in all aspects of the conduct of school business. However, as the number of education entrepreneurs has increased in recent years, so has the number of education snake oil dealers. The problem for school leaders is that sometimes it is very difficult to tell the difference. Box 3.1 contains an example.

Box 3.1

You receive a call from Sarah, the local representative of CognITSoft Systems, a software and curriculum publisher that has been in business about 8 years. You know Sarah because she used to teach fifth grade in your district and has worked as an instructor for the local university. Sarah tells you that her company has just released Reading for the World, an innovative reading and professional development program aimed at the middle school level. The program employs leading edge technology and a new multimedia approach to reading instruction for middle school. It includes a variety of World Wide Web-based, high interest activities for students and a series of colorful, culturally responsive classroom materials. When Sarah tells you that the program is "linked to our state reading standards," you get interested, because you know that too many seventh grade students in your district have been performing below standard in reading for the past 3 years on the statewide accountability test. But you get really excited when Sarah tells you that CognITSoft also is releasing the Reading for the World Professional Development Academy to accompany the student program. This package academy includes cyber-classes, in-person consultants, and a variety of attractive support materials geared toward beginning teachers and their mentors. Staff turnover is a problem in your district and administrators have been encouraged to implement teacher support and induction initiatives. The Reading for the World program seems like the perfect solution to your problems. The program is competitively priced, compared with other similar options on the market.

Should you buy the Reading for the World Program? What criteria should you use to decide? Let's look at some of the standards you could use:

- *Can you afford it?* Probably. CognITSoft no doubt has done extensive marketing research and is pricing the various components of the program at points that are consistent with the budgets of a majority of middle school reading programs.
- *Is it recommended by a trusted source?* Yes. You know Sarah as a sincere professional who believes in the product she is selling.
- *Does it meet a need?* Clearly. This program addresses two key areas of concern for you, middle school reading and new teacher development.
- *Does it have a solid reputation?* Hmm. . . . It's a new program using new technology and a new approach to instruction. You don't have much to go on here do you?

Box 3.2

Listed below are some instructional practices that were implemented in public schools in the not-too-distant past that we now know don't work:

- Early in the 20th century, seats and desks were bolted to the floor of classrooms. Then, in the 1960s and 1970s, school designers experimented with open designs in which classrooms were separated by moveable walls or even partitions. We now know that neither of these designs worked all that well.
- When we thought that learning disabilities were caused by deficits in sensory integration, many schools hired occupational and physical therapists to conduct sensory integration therapy. Students receiving this treatment were spun around on swings, walked on balance beams, and rolled around on therapy balls. We now know that sensory integration therapy doesn't have much effect on the academic performance of students with learning disabilities.
- The standard practice in reading classrooms has been, for years, ability-organized reading groups, where one student reads and the rest of the students in the group follow along and listen. We now know that students learn best when

(Continued)

(Continued)

instruction actively engages them and they receive effective feedback. Passively following along does little to improve the performance of beginning readers.

- When computers were first introduced into schools, they were perceived as specialized equipment that needed to be located in computer labs and computer skills were taught in isolation, separate from the rest of curriculum. These computer labs often remained empty for large parts of the school day and so the computers went unused. As the price of computers has steadily dropped, and as we have learned more about how to integrate computers into teaching and learning, we now know that it is better to distribute computers throughout the school building and use them as part of a specific curriculum.

- Age- and grade-equivalent scores are reported by most major test publishers and continue to be used widely to describe student performance. However, age- and grade-equivalent scores are based on the false assumption that learning progresses in a linear fashion from year to year. We all know that children learn in fits and starts, with big gains in some years and small gains in others. These scores have been widely discredited by all major educational and psychological professional organizations.

- Organizing high schools into ability tracks was an accepted practice for most of the 20th century. We now know that ability tracking benefits only the students in the very top tracks and works to the disadvantage of virtually everyone else in the school.

- At one time, children with disabilities were placed in state-funded residential institutions. Later, when the institutions were closed, children with disabilities were educated in separate schools and centers. Eventually, the number of students educated in these settings became very small and students with disabilities were educated in separate classrooms within the school. Now we know that all students in the school benefit when students who have disabilities are educated in general education classrooms with their peers.

All instructional practices are not created equally. The problem we face is that it is not always immediately clear from simply observing a classroom or talking to a teacher whether an instructional practice is likely to succeed. Practices that seem like a great idea at the time later turn out to be instructional bombs, while other practices that may seem, at first glance, unlikely to help children learn, turn out to be highly effective. Some approaches and strategies work well for some students but not others, and some instructional practices work for some teachers but not others. An alarming number of instructional practices found in schools today don't actually work too well for anyone.

What Are Proven Instructional Practices?

We said that building a high-quality program where all students are learning requires *proven instructional practices*. But just what are proven instructional practices? These are practices that have been subjected to scientific testing and found to be consistently effective. Proven instructional practices produce the kinds of effects they claim, across many applications.

> For a more in-depth analysis of what constitutes research-based practice, see the recent National Academy of Sciences report by Shavelson and Towne (2002).

Proven instructional practices have two key characteristics:

1. They have been validated by scientific studies.

2. They have been examined by the larger educational community.

Scientific Validation

Usually the process of verifying and validating the effectiveness of an instructional practice requires conducting multiple carefully controlled studies. In order to understand how rigorously researched a particular program or intervention may be you may need a brief review of some research principles.

There are two large categories of types of research: quantitative and qualitative. *Quantitative* research allows investigation of cause and effect relationships. Quantitative methods of data are necessary to answer questions such as "How did this specific instructional method affect students?" *Qualitative* research is appropriate when a researcher is searching for broader patterns or is seeking to situate an educational practice in a larger societal or policy context. Qualitative research can be

You can find more information about the standards for educational research at these Web sites:

The Action Evaluation Research Institute: www.aepro.org

Research Methods tutorial: www.camden.rutgers.edu/dept-pages/sociology/main.htm

U.S. Department of Health and Human Services, Offices for Human Research Protections: www.ohrp.osophs.dhhs.gov/irb/irb_guidebook.htm

appropriate to answer questions such as "How did a school go about implementing a new curriculum and what barriers did it face?" Neither approach to research is right or wrong. In fact, both types of research are necessary to make good choices about programs. What is important is that the research should be conducted in accordance with accepted scientific and ethical standards established by the major research organizations in our profession, such as the American Educational Research Association (AERA) and the American Psychological Association (APA). We now know that both qualitative and quantitative methodologies have a place in our profession.

Box 3.3   What's the Difference Between Qualitative and Quantitative Research?

Type of Questions

- Quantitative research generally involves very specific questions about relationships among larger groups or populations, for example, the reading achievement of first-grade students taught phonemic awareness or drop-out rates of Hispanic boys in high schools that have implemented high stakes testing.
- Qualitative research generally involves intense examination of a specific situation to address broad, nonspecific questions, for example the leadership style of three middle school principals or the cooperative culture in two urban third-grade classrooms.

Objectivity

- Quantitative research generally involves objective data-collection strategies and statistical analysis. For example, a researcher might collect reading test scores from a group of first graders who had been taught phonemic awareness and from a comparable group who had not been taught phonemic awareness and then compare these scores using analysis of variance (ANOVA).

- Qualitative research generally employs subjective data collection and analysis strategies. For example, a qualitative researcher might conduct a series of interviews with a small number of participants and then look for themes across those interviews.

Generalizability

- Quantitative studies attempt to control the influence of random events that are irrelevant to the central question being investigated. Therefore, quantitative researchers intend for the results of their studies to be applicable to all other situations that are similar to the one they have studied. For example, a quantitative researcher likely would expect that any findings about the reading achievement of the first graders in a particular study could be generalized to all first graders.
- Qualitative researchers make no claims of generalizability of their results beyond the specific situation they examine. For example, a qualitative researcher probably would not suggest that the leadership styles of the three particular middle school principals in a study would necessarily be similar to that of other middle school principals who were not in the study.

The Importance of Using Published Research

Scientific rigor also means that the results of research are reported and available for examination by the larger educational research community. Anecdotal reports of effectiveness do not constitute scientific scrutiny, nor do written reports or materials that have not been subject to outside review. Any practice that is called effective should be backed up with written descriptions of the supporting research that answers who, when, where, and what happened. Generally, this public reporting is accomplished through publication in credible research publications or sometimes through presentation of the results at research conferences.

In the not-too-distant past, educators relied primarily on scholarly journals to present findings of research. These journals contain articles written by experts or scholars in the field and are intended for other scholars and practitioners in the profession. The reason that many of these articles often are technical is that scientific rigor requires that research provide enough information to allow others to replicate the research. Articles published in scientific journals are reviewed by a board of knowledgeable scholars whose job it is to check the quality of the research. In contrast, articles in the popular press, such as magazines (paper or electronic), contain few if any references, often are written by journalists or laypersons who have little specialized knowledge of the topic, and are written for consumption by the general public. Many of the commercially available educational materials also do not contain any research or references to substantiate the product.

With the growth of the Internet, the sources of information about instructional practices have exploded. Reports of research about instructional practices are published routinely on the World Wide Web by government agencies, publicly funded research institutes, private foundations, professional organizations, and a wide variety of public and private special interest groups.

In the middle ground between scholarly journals and magazines are publications or Web sites devoted to the practical concerns of teaching or administering educational programs. Articles in practitioner journals tend to be more general than those in scholarly journals and written for a broader audience of practitioners in the profession who are not necessarily going to replicate a study. These publications can be useful for tracking trends or finding accounts of field-based applications of instructional practices. Regardless of the type of publication or medium you use you should look for certain critical information in order to judge the quality of a specific practice.

Standards for Evaluating the Quality of Research

The gold standard of educational research is *experimental* design in which subjects are randomly assigned to treatment and control groups. Well-designed experimental studies allow clear, unambiguous decisions about the effectiveness of an intervention, because all of the irrelevant factors that could affect the outcome of the study have been eliminated. Box 3.4 provides an example of an experimental study.

Box 3.4

Suppose you want to find out if using a word processor improves students' ability to revise second drafts of their papers. You decide to run an experimental study. First you randomly assign students to one of two treatments: the word-processing revising group and the paper-and-pencil revising group. Next, you provide the same writing instruction to both groups. After the instruction is complete, you give both groups a writing and revising task and see which group does better on some objective measure of organization, cohesion, and mechanics. Which group do you think would do better? Why?

(By the way, when Grejda and Hannafin (1992) did this experiment they found that using a word processor improved the writing of middle school students.)

Source: Grejda and Hannafin (1992).

Because experimental designs always involve random assignment of subjects to treatment and control groups, careful manipulation of treatment and control conditions, and use of a common measure of outcomes, we have much more confidence in the results of experimental studies than we do in other designs. For this reason, experimental studies are commonly used in medical research, where the costs of making a wrong inference on the basis of a study can be very high.

Of course, educational researchers can't always randomly assign students to separate treatment groups. There may be logistic or ethical considerations, or the instructional practice being studied may not lend itself to manipulation in an experimental study. You couldn't randomly assign students to a poor-reading-instruction group or a no-math-instruction group.

There are a variety of high-quality research designs that don't involve randomization. Indeed, most of the research that is done in education involves procedures that are not, strictly speaking, experimental. Other widely used and respected empirical research designs may involve surveys, interviews, observations, and case studies. In fact there are so many designs used in educational research that it can be difficult to decide whether a particular instructional intervention has been validated scientifically. However, there are some key features that all high-quality research has in common:

- *Peer Review*. Organizations and individuals who are honestly concerned with increasing the knowledge base in our profession are not afraid to subject their work to the scrutiny of *informed* peers in the profession. This is where examination by the larger educational community takes place. It is important to know your sources. Is the journal or publication you rely on to inform you of new practices using outside reviewers who are independently judging the quality of the research?

- *Representative Samples*. Quantitative research is premised on the idea that the results obtained from a small sample can be generalized or applied to a larger population. Therefore, it is a rule of thumb that the more a sample in a study resembles the students in your school, the more applicable the results of the study are for your students. For example, if your school includes a high number of students who speak Spanish as their first language, you would want to make sure that the instructional approaches you adopt in your school have been researched with Spanish-speaking students. Similarly, you might want to be sure that research was conducted in real classrooms with real teachers and not just at a laboratory school or in a highly controlled setting.

- *Adequately Sized Samples*. In addition to the characteristics of the study sample, you also should be concerned with the size of the sample. There is no single hard-and-fast rule for determining an adequate sample size, but in general, more is better. Most research designs require samples of at least 25 subjects in each group being examined. The exceptions to this rule are qualitative and single-subject studies, which often involve only a few subjects. In the latter case, you would want to see the same results achieved over multiple trials with different students.

- *Reliable and Valid Measures*. Most educational studies involve some sort of measurement system. For example, students in two different reading treatments might be given a reading test at the beginning and end of the study. It is critical that the measures used to evaluate an instructional approach meet the same standards of technical adequacy as we require of other testing systems in schools. The measures must have high *reliability* and must yield *valid* decisions about the variable being examined. We discuss these important concepts in more detail below.

- *Replication*. This means there have been multiple research studies in different contexts to find out if the same results are obtained. Usually, replication involves a different set of participants and often involves systematic change of some aspect of the original study, while retaining its essential elements. You should be suspicious when an instructional practice has only been investigated by one researcher or a few of that researcher's associates or if different researchers report drastically different findings about the practice. In general, when there are multiple replications of a study, with similar results, we can be confident that the finding is not an aberration. Similarly, when an instructional practice has been investigated by studies that employ different designs (for example, qualitative, quantitative, case study) and similar results are obtained, we can have more confidence that the practice is a sound one.

Quality of Evidence

It would be nice if the Consumers Union issued an annual buying guide for instructional practices and educational products to help educators make informed decisions about how and what to teach. Unfortunately, the responsibility for judging the quality of an intervention or product largely is left up to individual teachers and school leaders. There are two criteria educators can use to evaluate the quality of the evidence regarding instructional practices: quantity of evidence and credibility of evidence. Box 3.5 provides an example that illustrates these criteria.

Box 3.5   Two Dimensions for Evaluating Quality

In 1983, the Senate committee that oversaw the supplemental food program for Women, Infants, and Children (WIC) was confused by conflicting testimony it had been receiving about the effectiveness of the program. The committee chair, Senator Jesse Helms, asked the General Accounting Office (GAO) to conduct an evaluation of the methodological soundness and credibility of the claims of existing research evaluating the WIC program. Specifically, the Senate committee was interested in the impact of the WIC program on miscarriages, stillbirths, and infant birth weights. The research team at GAO located over 100 reports and studies investigating the WIC program but discovered that these studies addressed nearly 200 topics, such as transportation issues in WIC programs, the nutrition of pregnant mothers, and the length of time participants were enrolled in WIC, in addition to the central question of impacts on birth weight. Eventually, the team narrowed their attention down to the 51 reports that dealt directly with the issues of concern to the Senate. At the same time, the GAO team found that the quality of the studies ranged from very professional to very poor. Some of the reports included little or no data, while others employed high-quality research designs. To make sense of the WIC studies, the GAO team developed a two-dimensional evaluation system, with *quantity* of evidence on one axis and *credibility* of evidence on the other.

Source: Hunt (1997).

Figure 3.1 Quality of Studies and Credibility of Information

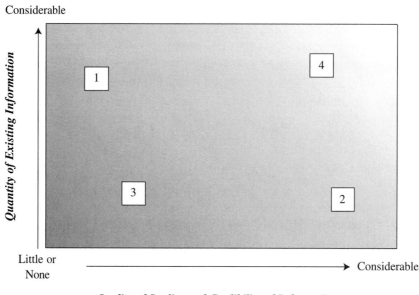

Considerable

Quantity of Existing Information

Little or
None

Considerable

Quality of Studies and Credibility of Information

Source: Adapted from U. S. General Accounting Office (1984, p. iii).

The chart shown in Figure 3.1 is similar to the one the GAO team eventually developed to display their evaluation scheme. The horizontal axis refers to the quality of the evidence that supports a practice, while the vertical axis refers to the quantity of information about the practice.

Some instructional practices are widely discussed in the professional literature and popular press, but have not been validated in studies that employ the standards of quality we discussed earlier. These studies would be found in the area marked by the "1" in the figure. It is difficult to tell if these practices are really effective or are simply a passing fad getting an inordinate amount of media attention. *Popular* isn't the same as *effective.*

Other practices may have been researched in very well-designed, high-quality studies, but only a few studies of the practice have been conducted. These practices *may* be effective, but much more replication is needed. Practices such as these would be found in the area marked by the "2" in the figure. New and emerging instructional practices that have not been validated in rigorous research and are not widely described in the literature would be found in the area marked by the "3" in the figure. Locally developed curricula and many classroom-based interventions would fall into this category. The most desirable combination of quality and quantity of evidence is represented by the area marked with a "4" in the figure. These are interventions that have been validated by rigorous research employing the standards we discussed earlier and have been widely described in the research literature. These are the interventions you generally will want to adopt in your school.

DATA-BASED DECISION MAKING

Throughout this book, we have emphasized that the key to ensuring the success of all children in your school is good problem solving. There are no one-size-fits-all answers. What works for one student or age group may not be right for another and what works in someone else's school may not be successful in yours. You need effective decision tools to determine what works and what doesn't. In Section II we presented decision frameworks for aligning IEPs with standards, for selecting accommodations and modifications, and for designing positive behavioral supports. Earlier in this section, we discussed the importance of selecting scientifically proven instructional approaches and for understanding the science underlying those approaches. However, even when you use systematic decision frameworks and select scientifically sound interventions, you still need to collect data to evaluate your decisions.

Box 3.6   The Data-Driven Compact Car

In the late 1950s a number of small European cars, such as Volkswagens, Saabs, Volvos, and Renaults, were beginning to make a dent in the U.S. automobile market. They were inexpensive, fun to drive, and relatively trouble free. U.S. car manufacturers decided they needed to offer their own compact cars. In 1960, after extensive market research and some reverse engineering, Chevrolet introduced the Corvair to compete primarily with the Volkswagen Beetle. Like the Beetle, it had a rear, air-cooled engine, fully independent suspension, and a unitized body. These were all firsts for an American car manufacturer. In 1961, Chevrolet introduced a Corvair station wagon, a van, and a pickup truck, mirroring the offerings of Volkswagen at the time. Chevrolet continued manufacturing Corvairs until the 1968–69 model year. Today, most people assume that Ralph Nader's book, *Unsafe at Any Speed*, detailing problems with the rear

(Continued)

(Continued)

suspension on the early models is what killed the Corvair. In fact, the suspension problems described in Nader's book were corrected by the 1964 model year and a 1972 report by the National Highway Safety Administration noted that the Corvair was as safe as most other cars on the road at the time. Chevrolet stopped making the Corvair because its own research department collected data that indicated consumers wanted bigger muscle cars like the Camaro and Corvette. Gasoline was cheap and growing baby-boomer families needed more room.

Data-based decision making brought the Corvair into existence and data resulted in its demise.

Data and information are powerful tools for school leaders who aim to create high-quality special education programs. ISLLC Standard I emphasizes that school leaders will understand and use a variety of information sources and will know how to collect and analyze data. Data-based decision making is central to a process of continuous improvement and it is absolutely necessary for the creation of high-quality special education programs.

As is the case with many tools, it takes skill and practice to use data effectively in making decisions. Being able to collect and analyze data isn't enough. Even the most experienced administrator can succumb to the perils of poor judgment using data for the wrong reason or going beyond one's data to make judgments that are not valid. To be an effective leader you also need to be an effective decision maker and know how to avoid common errors of decision. In this section, we'll provide strategies to help you master data-based decision making.

Converting Data to Information

When we refer to *data* in schools, we usually mean the results of measurements or observations, such as assessment scores; census, enrollment, or attendance rates; results of parent surveys; and a wide range of demographic data. Schools are data-rich environments. Decision makers must convert data into useful *information*. Data become information when they improve the knowledge of the people using the data so they are better able to make a decision. Principals need to know which data are important and which are not useful to their school improvement efforts.

To be useful for decision making, data must be as current as possible. This means the interval between when data are collected, analyzed, and

Box 3.7

Alyssa is the principal of Horizons Middle School. Four years ago she led the faculty in her school in developing a curriculum renewal initiative to better align the math and reading programs with state standards and assessments. The initiative included study groups in which small groups of teachers read and discussed various approaches to reading and math instructional research, thematic curriculum days, and team-building workshops for grade-level teams to improve planning and communication. Many of the teachers reported that they thought these processes were successful and the study groups are now a part of the ongoing work of the school. For the past three years, reading scores on the seventh-grade statewide reading assessment have improved, with about 5% more students meeting standards each year. However, math scores have not improved as dramatically. This past year, 20% of the seventh graders who took the test were at advanced or proficient levels, but over the past three years, about 8% fewer students have met the basic math standard. Alyssa has scheduled a half-day meeting with her faculty to discuss assessment scores and the curriculum renewal process.

Alyssa and the faculty at Horizons Middle School have some difficult decisions to make and the research about decision making suggests they will probably get it wrong. Chances are they'll attend to the wrong variables or misinterpret the information they have available to them.

What errors of judgment are Alyssa and her teachers on the verge of making? If you were planning the agenda for the Horizons Middle School meeting, what topics and activities would you include? Do you know how to avoid some common errors of judgment and decision making that Alyssa and her team are at risk of committing? After you read this section, return to this scenario and see if your advice to Alyssa and her team has changed.

evaluated must be as short as possible. Data-based decision making should be a continuous process in which principals and school improvement teams identify the goals and desired outcomes they wish to achieve, clarify the decisions associated with those outcomes, and then collect, interpret, and use data to make decisions. This process is illustrated in Figure 3.2.

Let's look at each of the steps in this process.

Figure 3.2   Continuous Data-Based Decision Making

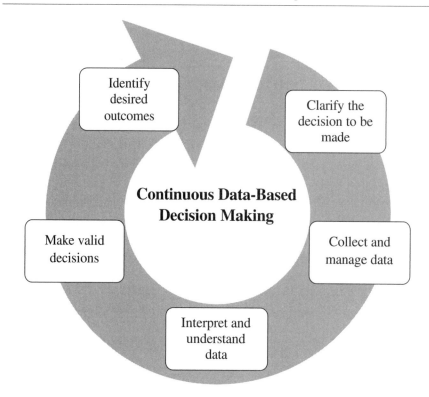

Identify Desired Outcomes

Decision making always is focused on a desired outcome. In schools, the outcomes with which we usually are concerned pertain to student learning. However, student performance is affected by a wide variety of school-level inputs, such as teacher expertise, curriculum materials, scheduling, use of paraprofessionals, and school climate. Think about Alyssa and the faculty at Horizons Middle School. What outcomes might they want to achieve? No doubt they want to increase the number of students who meet standards on the seventh-grade math assessment. But how should they do it? Should they work to improve teacher skills? Should they adjust the schedule to allocate more time to math? Should they deploy paraprofessionals differently to provide more specialized instruction for the students with greatest needs? Do they need to revamp the math curriculum?

As a rule, the process of identifying desired outcomes should focus on variables over which the decision makers have the most direct control, rather than those over which we can have relatively little impact. Principals can have direct control over how they allocate time and deploy teachers or curriculum resources. Teachers can choose instructional strategies, design activities and lessons, and organize and manage classrooms. Principals and teachers generally have much less control over things such as demographics, student mobility, legislated mandates concerning curricula and assessments, budget allocations, or community support for schools.

Principals should focus on information that most directly relates to students and classrooms. They should always consider the classroom-level effects of their decisions. To set clear priorities, start at the student and classroom level and move outward. This *proximal to distal* decision-making process is illustrated in Figure 3.3.

Think about the goal of increasing the number of students who meet proficiency on the math assessment. There is a variety of decisions a principal could make to try to accomplish this goal. For example, increasing the amount of time allocated to math instruction in the morning is a variable over which a principal probably has direct control and that would have direct impact on students. This decision would be located in the quadrant marked A in Figure 3.3. A decision that also might have a direct impact on students is to increase the amount of time spent on math homework. Of course, principals and teachers have less control over how and whether homework gets done. This decision would be located in quadrant D. A decision in the B quadrant might be to provide incentives for teachers to take math classes. The benefits of this decision for students likely would be less direct, depending on which math classes teachers take and the extent to which this decision increased math knowledge used in the school. A decision in the C quadrant might be to improve community attitudes about math learning. A principal would likely have relatively little impact over community attitudes about math, nor is it likely that this change would make much difference on student test scores.

The optimum distribution of decisions in the four quadrants in Figure 3.3 will vary from school to school. But, if you find that your school has difficulty meeting its goals, you should examine your priorities. If you find that much of your attention is focused on variables in the C quadrant, look for ways to move your decision making toward A.

Clarify the Decision to be Made

Once the desired outcomes for the decision process have been identified, you need to ask questions regarding the process:

1. Is this a decision that involves data and information?
Sometimes the decisions over which we agonize most are not those that can be answered with data. For example, despite research that shows that

Figure 3.3 A Decision-Making Framework

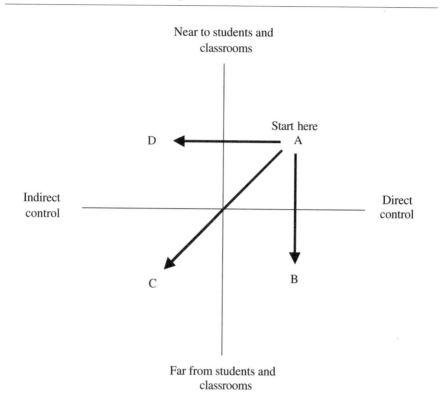

adolescent brain development makes it difficult for middle and high school students to do school work early in the morning, the school day in many high schools starts as early as 7:00 A.M. to accommodate bus schedules, not student development.

2. What information do we need in order to make this decision? Make sure the data you want to collect and the decision you are making match your desired outcome. For example, if you are evaluating schoolwide, classroom-based interventions, you need to make sure you focus on data collected at the classroom level, such as weekly curriculum-based measures, homework assignments, and time allocated to instruction. Data from the annual assessments probably will not be sufficient.

3. Who is going to make the decision? Be sure you are realistic about who ultimately has responsibility for the decision you want to make. Is it a decision that can be made at the classroom or grade level or does it involve the entire school or maybe central office? Don't ask your teachers to invest time and energy on a decision that ultimately will be made by someone else, including yourself. On the other hand, if the success of an initiative is going to depend on the buy-in of teachers and staff, don't exclude them from the decision-making process. Their participation, or lack of it, is in itself a decision.

   4.   *What kind of decision are we making?* There are three kinds of information-based questions that school leaders typically need to answer (Husen & Postlethwaite, 1994).

   a. *What happened?* questions are used to describe or evaluate *specific* programs or interventions. The data used to make these kinds of decisions are linked directly to a specific action being evaluated and generally will be collected in a particular classroom or school, rather than districtwide. For example, a high school principal might be interested in the effects of a schedule change on absenteeism among the current class of 10th-grade students, or a special education director might be interested in finding out if there are fewer new referrals in a particular middle school after a new schoolwide behavior management plan is implemented.

   b. *Why did it happen?* questions pertain to *cause and effect* relationships that may occur throughout an entire school or in schools across the district. For example, a curriculum coordinator may want to know *why* a reading program is more successful when implemented in second-grade classrooms than it is in third-grade classrooms or the personnel director may want to find out why there have been more requests for transfers among teachers in one middle school than in another one across town with similar demographics. The data needed to make these decisions generally must be collected from larger groups and often involve more than one measure.

   c. *Is there a trend?* decisions involve analysis of data accumulated over time to identify or clarify trends. Trend questions require data that have been collected and organized the same way for the entire time period being analyzed and generally involve data collected at the building or district level. It is important to remember that trend analysis does not necessarily answer cause-and-effect questions. For example, there may be a variety of reasons why the math scores of seventh-graders in a district have declined for the past 5 years. Math scores could be affected by curriculum, scheduling, the nature of the assessment system, or changes in demographics.

Collect and Manage Data

Data are collected and used for different purposes at different levels of the educational system. Continuous data-based decision making implies that you are matching the data you collect and use with the decision you are making. The most valid decisions are those that are based on information that is directly related to the decision.

Direct measures of student performance require lower levels of inference. The further removed the data are from the decision, the more susceptible the decision is to arbitrariness or error. For example, scores from the statewide reading assessment may be useful for evaluating the effects of a curriculum your district is using, but they wouldn't be sufficient for making referrals to special education. Low scores on the assessment might support the conclusion that the curriculum didn't work, but these same low scores would not necessarily support the conclusion that a student needs to be referred to special education because he or she has a disability.

Different assessments have different sensitivity to change. The smaller the changes you expect to see, the more sensitive your assessment tools need to be. For example, most statewide assessments are intended to measure big changes at the school or district level over a year's time, not small weekly or monthly changes at the student or classroom level. In fact, statewide assessments are rarely if ever useful for the day-to-day decision making that faces most school leaders.

To measure the effects of classroom-level interventions, you need to use classroom-based measures, administered weekly or monthly. To measure the effects of grade- or school-level interventions, you need to use grade-level measures administered monthly or quarterly. Examples of classroom or grade-level measures may include locally developed curriculum-based assessments, systematic assessment of student work, teacher ratings, and observations or periodic surveys. Table 3.1 shows some examples of data collection strategies and the frequency with which they are implemented.

Your data collection systems need to be efficient and be tailored to the specific contexts in your school and district. The more data collection is integrated into the day-to-day work of the school, the more efficient the process becomes. Also, a school with a higher population of non-English-speaking students may need to develop a variety of curriculum-based measures of math learning reflecting the languages spoken in the school. An English language, standards-based measure may miss improvements in math achievement actually being made in the school.

Data collection systems must meet minimum standards for technical soundness. *Reliability* is considered the minimally essential standard for determining data quality. Often, reliability is interpreted as relating to the

Table 3.1   Schedule for Using Progress Monitoring Tools

Frequency	Procedure	Purpose
Every two or three years	State mandated school accountability measures employing performance assessment and scoring rubrics	Evaluate school effectiveness at teaching curriculum standards and benchmarks
Once a year	Published, norm-referenced achievement tests	Compare students in a particular school or classroom with a national norm sample
Three to four times a year	Locally developed (district, school, or teacher) performance assessments linked to curriculum standards and benchmarks; use scoring rubrics and monitor individual student progress	Evaluate student use of complex thinking and problem solving contained in curriculum frameworks
Once a month	Curriculum-based measures of larger subcomponent skills such as written expression and math problem solving; use objective scoring procedures and decision rules	Monitor progress in skills that are subcomponents of larger curriculum outcomes
Once a week	Curriculum-based measures of basic skills such as oral reading fluency, math computation, or vocabulary; use objective scoring procedures and decision rules	Monitor progress in acquisition of basic skills associated with performance in larger domains

Source: Adapted from Nolet and McLaughlin (2000).

stability or consistency of a test or assessment procedure. We might say a test is reliable if it yields the same kind of results time after time. However, it is probably more appropriate to think in terms of the idea that underlies reliability: *random error.* Random error is the *static* or *noise* a data system contains that may decrease the validity of the inferences you make. The term *reliable* really means free from random error.

Random error is a fact of life: *All data systems contain random error.* The more random error a measure contains (i.e., is influenced by factors that are irrelevant to what is being measured), the less reliable it is. Think about the sources of random error in the following examples:

A seventh-grade teacher is administering an end-of-the-unit science test in her fourth-period science class. On the morning of the test, the annual candy bar sales fundraising campaign is launched at an all-school assembly. Does low performance on the test reflect students' science learning or the distraction of the assembly and sales campaign?

Your school district has targeted written expression as a priority area for improvement among elementary schools. There have been a number of teacher professional-development training academies, and several high-profile consultants have conducted workshops. The writing section of the statewide test is scored by panels of teachers who are paid to attend a week-long working retreat at a lakeside resort complex. Last year, a new contractor was hired to manage this scoring retreat and they changed the training and scoring protocols used by the previous contractor. Scores on the writing section for fourth graders were higher in 37% of the elementary schools in your district this year.

Because all data systems contain some amount of random error, no assessment task is completely reliable. Reliability is like happiness: it's always nice to have some, and the more you have, the better off you'll be. The prudent approach is to take as many steps as possible to ensure reliability during the planning, data collection, and analysis processes.

Interpret and Understand Data

The best data system in the world is going to be useless if the decision makers using it don't understand how to interpret the results. More important, data-based decision making should involve all of the stakeholders in your organization: teachers, administrators, paraprofessionals, parents, students, and community members. Therefore, you have roles to play relative to data: First, you must make sure you know how to make sense of data, and then you must make sure those with whom you work understand the data you want them to interpret. Here are some simple strategies for using data that can improve understanding.

Provide Clear Explanations. The data underlying most decisions in schools are relatively simple. They usually consist of scores that can be interpreted with some measure of central tendency (mean, median, mode), some measure of dispersion (range, standard deviation), or in terms of a ratio such as percentages. But even these common measures can cause confusion. Most teachers and many principals have had no more than one measurement course during their professional preparation. Most parents have had much less than that. Don't assume terms that are _used_ widely in schools to talk about assessments are necessarily widely _understood_. If you want the teachers and parents to participate in a data-based decision-making process, you need to provide clear explanations and definitions of the data you want them to use. A strategy that some school leaders have found effective is to provide a one-page glossary of measurement terms whenever data are being reported.

Use Off-the-Shelf Data Management Tools. The more specialized your data systems become, the more dependent you need to be on experts. Instead, look for ways to make every member of your school an expert in data utilization so they can incorporate a data-based decision-making approach into their day-to-day work. Choose data tools that are widely available and can be used readily by teachers, paraprofessionals, and parents. Spreadsheet programs such as Microsoft Excel come already installed on many desktop computers and can handle most data storage and analysis tasks at the school level. There are three related arguments for using generic data tools. First, they tend to be less expensive than specialized data systems to acquire and to maintain. Second, technical and educational support are widely available at low cost for most off-the-shelf systems. Third, because generic tools are widely available, many members of your faculty as well as parents may already know how to use them. For example, it is likely that there are teachers in your school district who are very skilled in the use of common spreadsheet software and can provide professional development or support colleagues as needed.

Keep It Simple and Flexible. Remember, the whole point of using data is to improve decision making. When data systems are unnecessarily complicated or specialized, it becomes more difficult to keep them updated, to extract useful information, or to see clear patterns, trends, and relationships. In general, you want to build data systems that can be updated easily and often and that can serve multiple decisions. Optimally, one should collect data at the lowest level of aggregation possible. Usually, this means you want data at the level of individual students. You can always aggregate up to the school level. You also want to analyze data at the lowest level of aggregation possible. Remember, you want to start your decision making at the student and classroom level and then move outward. The more you combine data across students and classrooms, across schools, and across significant subgroups, the more information you lose. Let the computer do the work of computing aggregate data when you need them.

Use Visual Displays. To understand data, a picture really is worth a thousand words. Whenever possible, present data using graphs and charts. Again, most off-the-shelf spreadsheet and word processing programs will have all the graphic tools you need. Never report data in

> Edward Tufte's reference books (1990, 1997, 2001) are excellent resources for strategies for displaying quantitative data.

only one format. If you report it in text, also include a graphic. If you report data in a table, try to find a way to also show it graphically. Use pie charts to show proportional data and bar charts to show central tendencies. Box plots can be used to show percentile ranks and dispersion, as well as change over time. Tufte (1997) recommends using visual displays of data for two tasks that are particularly important for data-based decision making: showing change and showing comparisons. Some examples of visual displays that accomplish these tasks are shown in Figures 3.4 to 3.8.

Box plots, such as the one in Figure 3.4, are useful for communicating a great deal of information in a simple graphic. With raw scores provided on the vertical axis, the box itself shows the range of scores between the 25th and 75th percentiles. The "whiskers" show the location of the 10th and 90th percentiles. The horizontal line within the box shows the median.

Time series data, such as those displayed in Figure 3.5, are useful for showing the progress of individual students. This graph shows the progress over 21 weeks for an individual student on a curriculum-based reading measure.

Time series data also can show both change and comparison for groups. Figure 3.6 shows drop-out rates for three groups of students attending Stanton High School for the past 12 years. This graph indicates that after a steady decline in the early 1990s, drop-out rates for all three groups have gradually increased in the past 7 years, with Hispanic students consistently dropping out at a higher rate than either white or African American students.

By organizing graphic displays of data into small multiples (Tufte, 1997) it is possible to compare the progress of a group of students or groups. Figure 3.7 shows the 21-week progress for six students who receive special education services for reading. Based on these data, do you think this is a successful special education program that is effective in improving reading?

Other types of graphic displays also can be presented in small multiples. Figure 3.8 shows the performance of fifth-grade students across the district, disaggregated by campus. At a glance, you can see which schools are in most need of assistance to increase test scores.

Make Valid Decisions

The quality of any decision depends directly on the quality of the information that is used to make the decision. The standard we use to

Figure 3.4   Third-Grade Reading Scores for 5 Years

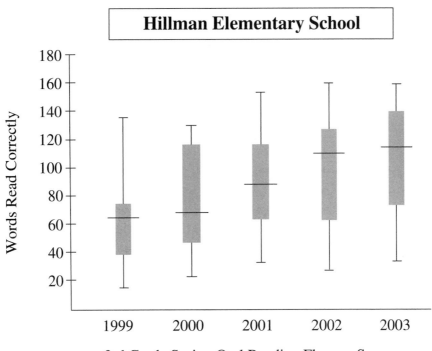

3rd Grade Spring Oral Reading Fluency Scores

Figure 3.5   Individual-Referenced Data Show Change Over Time

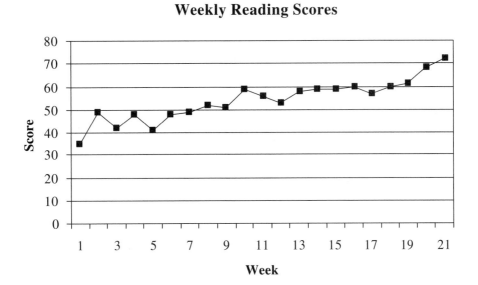

Figure 3.6   Drop-Out Rates at Stanton High School

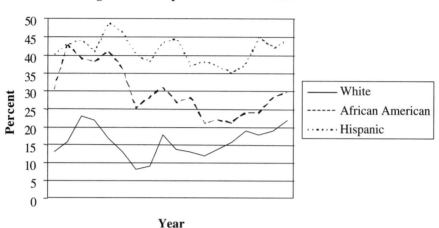

judge the quality of a decision is *validity*. While validity often is treated as an attribute inherent to tests, it is more accurate to refer to the validity of decisions based on some data or information.

Validity involves both data and logical reasoning. No matter how well intentioned, decisions that are based on bad data cannot be valid. Similarly, no matter how good the data are, they can still be used for bad decisions. For example, in many schools, when high-stakes testing is implemented and low scores are obtained, the initial response of administrators is to focus on superficial variables, such as teaching students how to take assessments, practicing items from old tests, or even providing orange juice and doughnuts to students to increase their energy before a test. Instead the focus should be placed on the systematic issues of curriculum and its alignment with what is being assessed and what teachers are teaching. The good data obtained from the assessment system are used to make bad decisions to fiddle around the edges rather than to tackle the substantial and more difficult work associated with improving student learning.

Validity is really more a relative than an absolute term: Some inferences are more or less valid than others, depending on the strength of the evidence supporting them. A decision is valid when it's based on evidence in the form of real data. Often it is a good idea to explicitly list the evidence that contributes to the validity of a decision. This makes it easier to involve all stakeholders in the decision process and to understand the reasoning used to arrive at a decision. Decisions based on meager evidence are the ones that ultimately cause the most difficulty and are the least valid.

(Text continues on page 79)

Figure 3.7   Small Multiples Show 21 Weeks of Data for Six Students

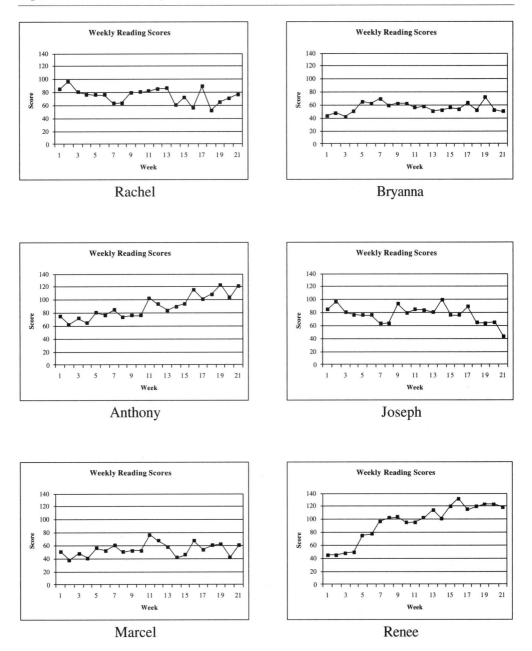

Weekly reading fluency scores for fourth grade students with IEP goals in reading.

Figure 3.8   2003 Assessment Results for All District Fifth Grades

2003 Assessment Results for All District 5ᵗʰ Grades

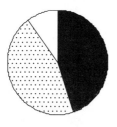

Delahandro Avenue Elementary

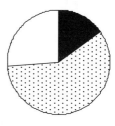

Rosa Parks Consolidated

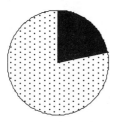

Lionel P. Reeves Elementary

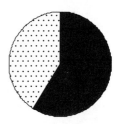

104ᵗʰ Street Elementary

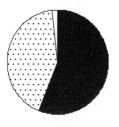

Marble Hollow Road Elementary

Sandra J. Bennett Elementary

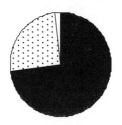

Ronald Reagan Elementary

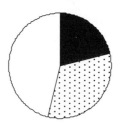

Madrona Technology Magnet

 Below Standard

At Standard

Exceed Standard

Recently, researchers have used the term *triangulation* to refer to the use of multiple methods of data collection from a variety of sources to obtain a more complete picture upon which to base inferences or decisions. The term suggests that it is possible to triangulate on the true state of affairs by obtaining multiple compass readings. Ideally, you would collect two forms of evidence: data that confirm the decision or course of action you plan to take and data that *fail* to confirm an opposing view or alternate decision. The idea is that if your decision is the right one, things that should go together do go together, and things that shouldn't go together don't.

Avoiding Errors of Judgment

Decision making is the process of choosing a course of action from among a set of alternatives. In an ideal world, we would be able to weigh the options objectively and arrive at a single best decision. Unfortunately, decisions pertaining to public schools often involve some degree of uncertainty, and, of course, usually the sources of uncertainty are far beyond our control. For example, changes in the economy can have a drastic affect on variables such as local school demographics, the availability of highly qualified teachers, and community support for bond issues. Similarly, changes in the political makeup of a state legislature or even local school board can have immediate impacts on a wide range of policies and priorities.

School leaders often need to make decisions on the basis of some information that they can neither look up nor calculate. For example, it might be necessary to estimate the size of next fall's kindergarten class, the performance of the seventh-grade class on the statewide assessment to be administered next spring, or the time needed to complete a curriculum revision project.

In the absence of a crystal ball, it is useful to have *heuristics,* or rules of thumb for decision making under uncertainty. However, heuristics are, by definition, imperfect rules, so it is important to know how much confidence to place in them to avoid making errors of judgment.

The Availability Heuristic. When asked to judge the frequency or likelihood of an event, people tend to be influenced by how *available* that event is in their immediate environment. This error may cause them to make inaccurate judgments about incidence or cause-and-effect relationships. For example, a principal who works in a school with a high percentage of native English speakers may underestimate the number of non-English speakers in the district. Similarly, a sixth-grade teacher whose class, by chance, contains many students with poor reading skills may lament the inadequacy of the reading instruction of the lower grade teachers.

The Representativeness Heuristic. Often, it is necessary to judge whether a particular event is an example or representative of some larger category of events or situations. The mistake people often commit is to make this decision on the basis of superficial or extraneous characteristics. Here are some examples:

A principal is interviewing a newly enrolled fourth-grade student and her mother. The mother speaks English with a heavy Central American Spanish accent, so the principal assumes that the family is poor and the student will need ESL services.

A teacher sees that a third-grade boy has poor handwriting and gets low marks on his spelling tests. She assigns the student to the low-middle reading group because she believes his handwriting and spelling make this student similar to students with poor reading skills.

A ninth-grade social studies teacher resists making accommodations for a student with a learning disability because he thinks the student just seems like a typical disorganized adolescent who needs to learn how to take more responsibility.

The *availability* and *representativeness* heuristics can be helpful when used in the presence of data. For example, if we want to know how likely it is that the fifth graders at your school will reach proficiency on the statewide assessment, you might consider the degree to which they represent the group of other fifth graders who met the standard on the test. To make that judgment, you would want to look at meaningful data pertaining to other assessments, curriculum alignment, and instructional variables in the classroom.

Unfortunately, once a decision has been made, people often resist adjusting that decision, even when additional data are present. Research has shown that decision makers tend to make only minor adjustments to an initial best guess, regardless of how inaccurate their original estimate is.

Of course, being conservative in adjusting initial decisions can serve us well. For example, a well-established method or belief should only be rejected when there is sufficient evidence that it isn't working. Yet, it seems that when an individual makes a judgment, his or her first estimate anchors the decision so firmly that the individual tends to make adjustments to the decision only grudgingly and tends to challenge the reliability or relevance of new information that supports a different decision. This phenomenon, known as *cognitive anchoring*, may be the single most difficult challenge to implementing a data-based decision-making system.

There is no foolproof way to avoid decision errors, but basing decisions on reliable data can help. By encouraging all members of your school to follow a data-based decision-making process, you can prevent some errors of judgment.

CREATING A COLLABORATIVE CULTURE

School leaders promote the success of all students by "advocating, nurturing, and sustaining a school culture and instructional program conducive to student learning and professional growth" (ISLLC, 1996). The key to realizing almost everything we've discussed in this book is creating a climate that supports teachers while promoting continuous improvement and new practices ("stroking and poking"). Leading for change is probably the most critical role of today's principal, and special education is among those programs that is experiencing some of the more significant changes, in terms of both policies and school-level practices. Today's school administrator must be a leader who promotes the success of all students, including those with disabilities, by facilitating the development and implementation of a vision of learning that is shared and supported by the school community.

As we noted at the beginning of this book, principals have often delegated responsibility for special education to a lead special education teacher or assistant principal. Delegating or distributing leadership for special education can be a perfectly good idea as long as the principal is fully accountable for the students who receive special education services and is aware of what constitutes special education practice. Principals need to ensure that special education students, teachers, and services are fully integrated into the vision and the ongoing operations of their school. Principals must ensure that students with disabilities are explicitly considered in school improvement planning and when they initiate new instructional initiatives and curricula. Principals must make certain that school improvement plans address the unique needs of these students and families and are based on disaggregated data. In short, principals must create a unified school in which special and general education teachers and other specialists work together to meet shared goals.

Special and general education collaboration is recognized as a necessary ingredient of most aspects of special education, including effective prereferral classroom interventions that prevent unnecessary referrals to special education, strategies that promote positive behavior and reduce discipline problems, and instructional practices that ensure that all students receive access to the same curriculum. Collaboration is a central feature in many of the IDEA requirements because there is solid evidence that collaboration results in better outcomes for students with disabilities.

For example, a number of studies have shown that teacher expectations about their students and their willingness to assume responsibility for the outcomes of their teaching have important consequences for learners. Research on school organization has pointed to the importance of fostering shared norms and values among teachers that emphasize academic growth and personal development for *all* students. For students who receive special education, it is often too easy for general educators to assume that they can't teach the student who has an IEP and that the student's low achievement or behavioral problems are just what are expected of a student with a disability. General education teachers also may not feel responsible for teaching these special children who are seen as requiring highly specialized instruction. Likewise, special educators can convey negative expectations to these students by trying to protect them from failure through reducing demands, dumbing down curriculum, and lowering standards.

Teachers communicate their attitudes toward individual students and these attitudes become part of the students' school culture. The attitudes influence a student's own beliefs about his or her abilities. Imagine how a student feels who each day must face classrooms where he or she not only struggles to make sense of the instruction but also perceives that the teachers do not believe that he or she can succeed. Over time these negative classroom and school cultures alienate and anger some students; some may act out, while others withdraw. Many of these students disengage entirely from school and eventually stop coming altogether.

Collaboration Between General and Special Educators

We know that general and special educator collaboration is a key feature of schools that work for students with and without disabilities. But, collaboration has proven to be particularly important in special education.

Collaboration and Exemplary Special Education

One example of the importance of general and special education collaboration can be found in several national projects funded by the Office of Special Education Programs to identify and study schools that were "Beacons of Excellence" for all students. A total of 10 Beacons schools, including elementary, middle, and high schools, were identified across

---

Box 3.8   General Education Teachers' Role in Special Education

---

- 96% of all students with disabilities are educated in regular school buildings and 47% spend less than 21% of their day outside of general education classrooms (U.S. Department of Education, 2002).
- 96% of general educators currently teach students with disabilities or have done so in the past.
- General educators have an average of 3.5 special education students assigned to their caseload.
- The most common disabilities represented on general educators' caseloads are specific learning disabilities, speech or language impairments, and emotional disturbances; however, 1 in 10 general educators have caseloads that include students with other health impairments, mental retardation, hearing impairments, or developmental delay.

Source: SPeNSE (2001).

---

the country that were obtaining exemplary results for both special and general education students. These were intensively studied over 3 years to identify key indicators of success. Across all sites a common set of characteristics were identified, including the following:

- A clearly defined core curriculum and set of performance standards that *every* teacher understood and could articulate. At the high-school level this was specific to a subject matter area, whereas elementary and middle school faculty shared an interest in the total curriculum.
- Clear annual school-improvement targets based on student data that included student performance on assessments disaggregated between and within specific groups, including students with disabilities, and parent and community perceptions of the school. While these data were common across schools, each school also collected and analyzed other data, such as disciplinary referrals, which were critical to an individual school's improvement. The principal, along with the faculty in each of these schools, carefully

examined data to design interventions to monitor improvement efforts.

- Expectations that every teacher contributes to achieving the school improvement goals and must be involved in the overall school improvement process. Often working in cross-disciplinary teams, teachers collected and examined data and developed goals and strategies and joint professional development opportunities.

- Time and opportunity through a variety of venues to problem solve and share ideas and strategies—both in small groups and between two individuals.

- A shared and common language among teachers that results from shared goals for improving the performance of all students.

- Clearly articulated and shared expectations that *every* child in the school can achieve at higher levels and that achievement valued. Teachers also believe that they can improve every student's performance.

- Students and families are not blamed for low achievement and no teacher abdicates responsibility for teaching the general curriculum because a student has an IEP or receives special education. *All* teachers accept responsibility for helping *all* students progress to and achieve higher levels. There was no "your student" or "my student," but "our student."

- There is no one way to collaborate, nor do all collaborating schools look the same.

Coteaching and Collaborative Consultation

There are several different ways that special and general education teachers collaborate within schools and classrooms. But coteaching and collaborative consultation are probably the most common. An important feature of both of these approaches is the emphasis on equality between teachers in terms of responsibilities and roles. Both also require shared problem solving and planning.

Collaborative Consultation

Collaborative consultation can take several forms but differs from the *expert-novice* or directive consultation approach that we often see in education. In almost all situations teachers find the directive expert model of consultation to be not very effective. Often the solutions to problems presented by individual students require some change in what

Box 3.9   Lessons From Beacons of Excellence Schools

Key Indicators of a Collaborative School

- Special education is not a place or a parallel program. Students with disabilities and special education teachers are fully integrated into classrooms and the school.
- There is one curriculum aligned with standards and all staff understand the curricular goals.
- Every student's IEP is guided by the state curriculum standards and performance expectations.
- Special and general education teachers and paraprofessionals work together to design accommodations and modifications and provide individualized instruction to help students with disabilities access the general curriculum.
- General and special education teachers have the time, support, and flexibility needed to collaborate in a variety of ways. In general, special educators provide specific accommodations and specialized instructional strategies and the general education teacher guides instruction in subject matter content.
- Related services, particularly speech and language therapists, provide therapy that is both integrated into and supports the curriculum and meets individual student needs.
- Open and ongoing communication between teachers and parents is expected and supported by the principal.

Box 3.10

Valerie Lee, an educational researcher at the University of Michigan, along with her colleagues, has studied the impact of school culture and teacher expectations on student achievement. Her research points to the importance of having teachers assume personal responsibility for student achievement as well as for all faculty in a school to share what she calls *collective responsibility* for the achievement of all children. This research has demonstrated that in schools with high levels of collective responsibility where there are consistent attitudes and expectations among faculty, students learn more in all subjects. Lee has devised a collective responsibility scale that can measure the degree to which a school's faculty shares a common commitment to student achievement. See, for example, Lee and Loeb (2000).

a teacher is doing. A teacher may have to change some aspect of his or her instruction or classroom organization or may have to provide more intensive instruction. Directing someone to teach differently is not effective. Working with someone collaboratively to assess educational problems, design interventions, and then supporting them as they try out their solutions results in change. The key to successful collaborative consultation is to strike the right balance between providing new information or skills and engaging in mutual problem solving that allows the individual teacher to choose and adapt solutions. However, in some cases a specialist may be required to diagnose a particular condition and propose a specific treatment or provide information about new instructional intervention.

A number of *collaborative* consultation models have been successfully implemented in schools to assist teachers with students who are experiencing academic or behavioral problems. Often these approaches have been used to prevent inappropriate referrals to special education. These consultation teams have many names, such as teacher assistance team, prereferral intervention team, and instructional consultation team. They almost always involve teachers, school psychologists, counselors, and other specialists as needed.

The effectiveness of these consultation models can vary greatly across schools. Much depends on how well the model is implemented and research has shown that without close monitoring few work well as a means of reducing referrals to special education. Effectiveness depends on the buy-in of individual teachers and their willingness to trust the team, problem solve with the team, and make a sincere and sustained effort to implement specific interventions. Some of the major reasons that collaborative consultation teams fail to resolve individual student problems and/or reduce unnecessary referrals to special education are the lack of specificity regarding the student's problem, lack of sufficient expertise among team members with respect to providing differentiated instructional strategies and curriculum adaptations, lack of data on the success of the model, and lack of follow-through on the part of the referring teacher.

Consultation teams must have the collective expertise to carefully isolate and document the students' learning or behavior problem that has prompted a teacher to seek help from the team. This means listening to the teacher as well as collecting data on the student's actual behavior or performance. Both formal and informal assessments of student skill levels or other behaviors are required as discussed earlier in this section.

A team must also be able to generate workable solutions. This requires mutual problem solving using the data, as well as access to specialists in curriculum and behavior. Teams that rely on the same collection of favorite instructional tricks or strategies, without understanding the exact nature of a student's problem, are dispensing information but not real solutions. These teams are not effective and too often become a pro forma step on the way to a special education referral or source of frustration to referring teachers.

The problems described above are also likely to contribute to the most common reason that the various consultation teams fail, which is lack of follow-through on the part of the referring teacher. Individual teachers who seek help with a particular student need to be invested in solving the problem *and* they need to believe that the solutions to the problem are within their capacity to implement. Principals can be very important in communicating to a teacher the expectation that he or she engage in serious problem solving and consultation and be committed to using the teams' recommendations.

Principals also ensure that consultation teams are supported. Teams need sufficient time to engage in discussions with one another as well as with parents and other experts. Teams may need access to experts or specific information to help them design interventions and they need to see that their activities are valued and yield results in terms of improved student achievement or behavior.

Special and General Coteaching

An increasingly common collaboration model is coteaching between general and special educators. As the name implies, coteaching means at least one general and one special education teacher together providing instruction to a group of special and general education students in the same classroom. The principles of coteaching are similar to team teaching with the exception that the special educator's *primary* responsibility is to ensure that students with disabilities in the classroom are accessing the general education curriculum and otherwise working toward the goals of their IEPs. The coteaching model offers opportunities to meet the needs of a diverse group of students. Research is not definitive on the effectiveness of coteaching. In part, this is due to the various approaches to coteaching.

Marilyn Friend and Lynne Cook (1996) describe five approaches to coteaching: (1) one teaching–one supporting, (2) station teaching, (3) parallel teaching, (4) alternative teaching, and (5) team teaching.

One teaching–one supporting is the most common form of coteaching and may be the easiest to implement. In this model, one teacher has the primary role of designing and delivering instruction while the second teacher floats, helping and observing individual students. A major downside to this model is that too often it is based on having all children learn the same content in the same manner. This means that the special educator's role is to help students keep up or catch up, rather than to design individualized accommodations or differentiate instruction. In some coteaching classrooms, the special education teacher begins to function almost like an instructional assistant acting totally under the direction of the general educator. Aside from the inequities in roles that this approach to coteaching may create, it does not provide opportunities for much differentiation in instruction or for more intensive instruction. The one teaching–one supporting approach to coteaching can be an acceptable approach in some instructional situations, such as when introducing a new concept, but only if both teachers engage in designing and implementing the lesson.

In *station teaching*, general and special education teachers divide the content of a lesson and each is individually responsible for planning and teaching aspects of the lesson to some part of the class. Every student in the class moves through both teacher-led groups. Each teacher teaches every student but in smaller groups. In this model, the special educator functions like another teacher in terms of his or her responsibility for the curriculum. However, this approach, if used exclusively, can fail to provide the differentiated instruction or the more intense instruction that students with disabilities require.

Parallel teaching occurs when the class is divided and each teacher delivers the same content and instruction to his or her section of the class. This type of coteaching is best for drill exercises or when the content is limited to a few key facts or knowledge so that instruction for both groups of students can be similar. Again, parallel teaching can result in a lack of differentiation or additional support needed by certain students.

Alternative teaching is probably the second most common form of special and general education coteaching. In this model, special and general educators jointly plan instruction, but the special educator focuses on reteaching or reinforcing materials taught, differentiating instruction, and making curricular accommodations and modifications for small groups of students with and without disabilities who may need extra assistance. This model can be flexible and permits any student who may need some additional help to receive some additional instruction.

In implementing alternative teaching it is important not to stigmatize students who may be in the group receiving the different instruction. It is also essential that special and general education teachers be clear about the core and essential knowledge that is the object of the particular lesson.

Both teachers need to be focused on the key curriculum goals that their group of students is expected to learn.

Team teaching is a well-known strategy in general education and requires equal planning and equal roles in implementing instruction. In fact, in a team teaching arrangement, individual teams may use all or any of the strategies discussed above. Teachers trade off roles and groups of students.

Box 3.11

According to Friend and Cooke (1996), the most common complaints from teachers about coteaching are

- Lack of adequate time to talk and plan
- Lack of mutual respect
- Lack of shared goals or objectives for students in the class
- Lack of conflict resolution and communication strategies
- Inequity in task distribution

Creating a Collaborative Culture in Your School

Any or all of the above approaches will be effective only if the collaborating teachers have equal status in the classroom and recognize what knowledge and skill each brings to the collaborative effort. General and special education instructional collaboration requires sound knowledge of the curriculum and how to assess student skills and to monitor progress, as well as a range of strategies that differentiate instruction for individual students.

However, there are some cautions for principals when considering collaborative approaches. First, neither schools nor individual teachers should become locked into one approach to collaboration. More important, general education teachers should not depend solely on having a special education teacher in the class in order to be responsible for instructing the students with disabilities. Principals are essential to creating a collaborative environment. They must set the expectations that all teachers are responsible for all students. They should support and encourage a variety of collaborative instructional approaches. They also need to help teachers with the logistics of collaboration and provide individuals or a whole faculty with the professional development they require to build their collaborative skills.

Summary

In this book we have provided an introduction to the foundations of current special education practice. We have deliberately not focused on legal procedures because we believe that today's principal needs much more than a set of rules in order to be an effective leader for special education. Also, specific procedures and rules are determined state by state and district by district. We assume that any principal who is truly interested in becoming a more effective leader will be able to follow his or her district's procedures. We want principals to focus on instruction and results for students.

We have been influenced in our thinking by our own experiences in schools and by the *Standards for School Leaders* (ISLLC, 1996) that have been developed to guide the education and training of school administrators. The standards, which we refer to throughout this book, emerged from a model of school leadership that recognizes the complexity of today's schools but also believes strongly that, "Effective school leaders are strong educators, anchoring their work on central issues of learning and teaching and school improvement. They are moral agents and social advocates for the children and the communities they serve. Finally, they make strong connections with other people, valuing and caring for others as individuals and as members of the educational community" (p. 5).

Today's principal must promote a vision of learning that is shared and supported by the school community. It is not enough to simply accept special education students and classrooms into your building. You must understand what it means to *believe* in the educability of all, to *ensure* that each child has an equal opportunity to access the same critical knowledge and skills, and to be accountable for every child.

The principal provides the vision and the support to every member of the school to focus on curriculum and instruction. The principal creates an organization that is neither rigid nor allows complete autonomy among teachers. The principal provides multiple opportunities for all staff to learn how to help all students achieve at new and higher levels.

A principal does not just follow; a principal questions and understands. He or she makes decisions based on valid information supported by research and current policy. Above all, a principal is fair and ethical.

So, let's return to Mr. Baker and his middle school. Now that he has learned some important characteristics of special education, how might he respond to the question he had about special education students in his building?

Mr. Baker always understood that the IEPs of the students with disabilities in his school were very important documents. But he now has a better understanding that those IEPs should directly relate to the curriculum and have a particular focus on raising student achievement in reading, writing, and mathematics where test scores indicate the biggest deficits for students with disabilities.

Mr. Baker first assembles his special education teachers to review the most recent assessment data and leads a discussion about how they think the IEPs connect to the assessment data. His teachers's thoughts are ambiguous and conflicted. Some believe they should focus more on skill areas they have identified using their own assessments. Others feel that some of these students would benefit more from learning functional skills. The teachers definitely feel the competing priorities, and Mr. Baker helps the teachers understand the curriculum and the standards. He also visits classrooms to see how students with disabilities are receiving instruction in reading, writing, and math. He finds a very mixed bag in terms of instruction. Some students with disabilities are being instructed in the core content areas by special education teachers who are using a variety of commercial and teacher-made materials, including some reading materials and textbooks they have obtained from the elementary school. A group of sixth- and seventh-grade special education students are enrolled in general education math and science classes that are cotaught by the sixth- and seventh-grade math and science teachers. Other special education students are in general education classrooms with paraeducators assigned to them or with no visible support.

Mr. Baker understands that students with disabilities require individualized instructional arrangements, but he is not so sure that the arrangements are really a reflection of what the students need instructionally nor whether they are effective. The multiple arrangements seem to be a result of staffing and logistics, and he cannot find any data to suggest that teachers are monitoring the effects of any of these approaches. Also, instruction seems loosely coupled to the curriculum and the performance standards. Special education teachers support the time spent in general education classrooms and are proud of the inclusion they have achieved.

Mr. Baker decides that the effort to improve the scores of students with disabilities is going to be a complex task and will involve the entire school staff as well as the parents and families of the students who are receiving special education. He begins by collecting more data.

First, he administers a brief anonymous questionnaire to all of his teachers, asking them to what degree they feel responsible for the achievement of all students and for the behavior of all students. He also asks them to list their top three instructional concerns. To his surprise he finds a marked difference between his general and special educators in terms of the degree to which they perceive that everyone is responsible for all students. Special education teachers believe that they alone are responsible for students with disabilities. They also list lack of appropriate curricular materials, particularly textbooks; lack of parental cooperation and involvement; and lack of cooperation of general education teachers among the top three issues. General education teachers list lack of support for difficult students, lack of parental support, and homework.

Using this information, Mr. Baker brings together a group of general and special education teachers, the school's psychologist, and his assistant principal. Mr. Baker presents the following issues that he wants the team to address: poor assessment and the disconnect between special and general education instruction and teachers. He asks the team to help develop a set of goals to address the issues and to develop a schoolwide plan to meet the goals. He emphasizes the need to focus on professional development.

Mr. Baker's vision for his middle school is one in which special education students access and continuously progress in the general education. The evidence of this will be improved scores on the state tests and individual student curriculum-based assessments. Mr. Baker's vision also includes special and general education teachers working in tandem to improve the learning outcomes of all students in his school.

To accomplish this vision, Mr. Baker knows that his faculty must share a common language about curriculum and instruction. They must share common goals for improving the programs in the school and share responsibility for meeting these goals. Professional development must be designed by and include all teachers and in some instances families.

And, of course, throughout this journey of school improvement, Mr. Baker and his staff must carefully and continuously monitor progress toward the goals. Teacher attitudes, student learning and behavior, and parental perceptions of school climate are all important elements to be monitored.

Mr. Baker understands that quality special education services cannot be created or sustained in isolation within a school. Mr. Baker's commitment to effective leadership and adherence to the principles of school leadership means that he holds high standards for each child and believes in the power of a collaborative organization to make education successful for children.

In summary, Mr. Baker holds the new vision for special education leadership.

References

Friend, M., & Cook, L. (1996). *Interactions: Collaboration skills for school professionals* (2nd ed.). White Plains, NY: Longman.

Grejda, G., & Hannafin, M. J. (1992). The effects of word processing on the revisions and holistic writing of sixth graders. *Journal of Educational Research, 85,* 144–149.

Hunt, M. H. (1997). *How science takes stock: The story of meta-analysis.* New York: Russell Sage Foundation.

Husen, T., & Postlethwaite, T. N. (Eds.). (1994). *International encyclopedia of education* (2nd ed.). Oxford, UK: Pergamon.

Interstate School Leaders Licensure Consortium [ISLLC]. (1996). *Standards for school leaders.* Washington, DC: Council of Chief State School Officers.

Karger, J., & Pullin, D. (2002), *Exit documents and students with disabilities: Legal issues.* College Park, MD: Educational Policy Research Reform Institute, University of Maryland. Available at www.eprri.org.

Lee, V. E., & Loeb, S. (2000). School size in Chicago elementary schools effects on teachers' attitudes and students' achievement. *American Educational Research Journal, 37,* 5–31.

McGregor, G., & Vogelsberg, R. T. (1998). *Inclusive schooling practices: Pedagogical and research foundations: A synthesis of the literature that informs best practices about inclusive schooling.* Baltimore: Paul H. Brooks.

Moore, C. (1998). *Educating students with disabilities in general education classrooms: A summary of research* [Monograph]. Eugene, OR: Western Regional Resource Center.

Nader, R. (1965). *Unsafe at any speed.* New York: Grossman.

Nolet, V., & McLaughlin, M. J. (2000). *Accessing the general curriculum: Including students with disabilities in standards-based reform.* Thousand Oaks, CA: Corwin.

Oswald, D. P., Coutinho, M. J., & Best, A. M. (2002). Community and school predictors of overrepresentation of minority children in special education. In D. Losen & G. Orfied (Eds.), *Racial inequity in special education.* Cambridge, MA: Harvard Education Press.

Shavelson, R. J., & Towne, L. (Eds.). (2002). *Scientific research in education, committee on scientific principals for education research.* Washington, DC: National Research Council. Available at the National Academies Press Web site www.nap.edu/catalog/.

SPeNSE. (2001). *Fact sheet: General education teachers' role in special education.* Gainseville, FL: Author. Retrieved August 24, 2003, from www.spense.org.

Sugai, G., & Horner, R. H. (2002). Introduction to the special series on positive behavior support in schools. *Journal of Emotional and Behavioral Disorders, 10,* 130–135.

Thurlow, M. L., Elliott, J. L., & Ysseldyke, J. E. (1998). *Testing students with disabilities: Practice strategies for complying with district or state requirements.* Thousand Oaks, CA: Corwin.

Tufte, E. R. (1990). *Envisioning information.* Cheshire, CT: Graphics Press.

Tufte, E. R. (1997). *Visual and statistical thinking: Displays of evidence for making decisions.* Cheshire, CT: Graphics Press.

Tufte, E. R. (2001). *The visual display of quantitative information* (2nd ed). Cheshire, CT: Graphics Press.

U.S. Department of Education. (2001). *Twenty-third annual report to Congress on the Individuals with Disabilities Education Act.* Washington, DC: Author.

U.S. Department of Education. (2002). *Twenty-fourth annual report to Congress on the implementation of the Individuals with Disabilities Education Act.* Washington, DC: Author.

U.S. Office of Special Education Programs. (2003, Spring). Paraeducators. *Research Connections in Special Education, 12.* Available at ericec. org/osep/recon12/rc12cov.html.

Wallace, T., Pickett, A. L., & Liken, M. (2002, Fall). Feature issue on paraeducators supporting students with disabilities and at-risk. *Impact, 15*(2). Available at ici.umn.edu/products/newsletters.html.

Glossary of Selected Terms

Access to the General Education Curriculum   The IDEA requires that IEP teams consider how each student who receives special education will access and progress in the general education curriculum, defined as the content and instruction delivered in general education classes. Students with disabilities are to access the curriculum regardless of the setting in which they are being educated.

Accommodation   A device or support that is provided to a student with a disability in instruction and during assessments that is intended to offset the impact of the disability. An accommodation is not to change the construct being measured or taught or to lower the performance standard.

Action Research   A process in which principals and teachers study their own schools and classrooms with the goal of improving their professional practice.

Adaptation   Sometimes used instead of *modification*, it implies that general education content or instruction has been altered in some way for one or more students. It usually means that content or performance standards have been changed.

Alternate Assessment   Permitted under both IDEA and NCLB, these assessments are to be administered to students with disabilities for whom the general state or district assessments are not valid or do not reflect the curriculum of the child. These are intended for 1% or fewer of the students with disabilities.

Applied Research   Research that applies or tests theory to solve real-world problems. Applied research is rigorous and employs scientific methods, but it is not primarily concerned with building new theoretical constructs.

Assistive Technology   Any tool, device, or piece of equipment that can increase or improve the ability of a student with a disability to perform functions of daily living, including those involved with learning.

Availability Heuristic   An error of judgment often made by decision makers attempting to judge the frequency or likelihood of an event. People making this error tend to be influenced by the *availability* of that event in their immediate environment, which causes them to make inaccurate judgments about incidence or cause-and-effect relationships.

Behavior Disorders   Often used interchangeably with *emotional disturbance* or *emotionally handicapped* to mean students whose primary disability is in the area of adjustment and social and behavioral skills. Some states and professionals use this term in place of emotional disturbance because they believe it to be more descriptive of the nature of the students' disabilities.

Behavior Modification   Specific procedures used to manage or eliminate unacceptable behaviors. The procedures are based on principles of behavioral psychology and involve identification of specific behaviors that are to be changed and systematic application of consequences, either positive or negative, that will reduce the behavior.

Cognitive Disability   Often used to refer to students with mild to very marked mental retardation. A cognitive disability reflects limits in performing cognitive tasks, including but not limited to areas of memory; learning new tasks; making associations between events, facts, or concepts; and drawing inferences; as well as limits in *adaptive behavior* or the skills required for daily living.

Collective Responsibility   A term first coined by Dr. Valerie Lee to reflect the degree to which teachers perceive that their colleagues in their school share responsibility for the achievement of all students. High collective responsibility ratings among teachers have been correlated with higher levels of achievement.

Consultation   Two or more teachers and other professional staff engaging in planning and problem-solving discussions usually around a single child or a small group of children that is experiencing learning or behavior difficulties.

Coteaching   A model of classroom instruction in which special and general education teachers share instructional responsibilities within the same classroom. There can be several types of coteaching arrangements within a room. The key feature is that both the general and the special education teacher have equal responsibility and authority for planning and implementing instruction.

Data   The numerical results of measurements or observations. In schools, data usually refer to assessment scores; census, enrollment, or attendance rates; results of parent surveys; or a wide range of demographic indicators.

Decision Rules   Rules that are established ahead of time that guide a decision when it is needed. Decision rules often are used to assist with interpretation of data.

Experimental Design Research   Systematic scientific inquiry in which at least one independent variable is manipulated and other variables are held constant or controlled. The effect of this manipulation is then observed on one or more dependent variables.

Free and Appropriate Public Education (FAPE)   This is the basic legal entitlement of each child with a disability who is determined to be eligible to receive special education. The term *appropriate* is interpreted to mean that each child with a disability must have an individual educational plan designed by a team of individuals including the child's special and general education teacher and parents.

Functional Behavioral Analysis (FBA)   This approach to problem behavior is required under the IDEA for children who are known to have behavior problems but also in conjunction with the IDEA discipline requirements. (For a complete description of these requirements, see cecp.air.org/fba/problembehavior2/method2.htm.) A FBA requires that the IEP team look beyond the behavior that a child is exhibiting to identify specific correlates or causes of that behavior as well as conditions that seem to maintain or support the behavior. The purpose is to develop a comprehensive plan that will address the causes and consequences of problem behaviors and not simply be reactive.

Inclusion   This term can have varied meanings, although the core of inclusion is that every child with a disability is expected to be educated within a regular public school in natural proportions. That means that students with disabilities should be in their home school and not comprise more than approximately 10% of a school's population. Inclusion is also interpreted to mean that a student with a disability receives 80% or more of his or her education within the general education classroom.

Individualized Education Program (IEP)   Each child with a disability who qualifies for special education or related services is entitled to an IEP.

This is a personalized plan that directs the child's education. The IEP specifies annual goals and objectives and a description of the services that will be provided to enable the student to accomplish those goals. The IEP also must include a statement of the student's current educational performance and a description of any accommodations or modifications that may be required to enable participation in district or state assessments. The IEP is not a contract but it is a legal document that holds the school accountable for providing educational services that are likely to enable the child to progress in the general education curriculum.

Individuals With Disabilities Education Act (IDEA)   This is the federal law that governs how special education is to be defined and implemented within individual states. This name was given to PL 94-142 in 1990. Sometimes individuals refer to *IDEA'97* in reference to the number of new provisions that were added to the federal law when it was reauthorized in 1997. The law is periodically reauthorized and provisions may be altered.

Information   Data summaries, reports, graphs, tables, or descriptions that improve the knowledge of the people using it so they are better able to make a decision. Principals need to know which data are important and which are not useful to their school improvement efforts. Only those data that improve decision making would be considered information.

Learning Disabilities   Sometimes referred to as *specific learning disabilities*, this is one of the federal categories of disability eligible to receive special education under the IDEA. Students with this disability also represent the largest proportion (over 50%) of all students who are receiving special education. While criteria for defining a learning disability can differ by state, the underlying concept is that the child exhibits a difficulty in learning academic tasks such as how to read, write, or do math that is unexpected or unexplained by the child's cognitive level, educational experiences, language, or culture.

Least Restrictive Environment (LRE)   A requirement in the IDEA that, "to the maximum extent appropriate, children with disabilities. . . . are educated with children who are not disabled; and . . . removal of children with disabilities from the regular educational environment occurs only when the nature or severity of the disability of a child is such that education in the regular classes with the use of supplementary aids and services cannot be achieved satisfactorily" (§612(a)(5)(A)). The federal government measures LRE in terms of the percentage of time that students with disabilities are educated outside of general education classrooms (e.g., more than 60%, 21%–60%, 21% or less), or in separate schools, residential facilities, and home or hospitals. The IDEA regulations state that school districts make available a continuum of placements or settings.

Mainstreaming   This is another term that pertains to LRE and has traditionally been used to refer to students with disabilities moving from a special education class into a general education classroom or other setting such as the lunchroom or recess. Mainstreaming differs from inclusion in that it assumes that a student with a disability is assigned to a special education classroom and only leaves for certain times or certain activities. Inclusion assumes that a student with a disability is assigned to a regular classroom and is a member of that class and may only leave that setting for a specific activity.

Modification   This term refers to adjustments that are made to curriculum or assessment that alters either the construct being taught and assessed or the level of performance expected.

Office of Civil Rights (OCR)   An office within the U.S. Department of Education that is charged with ensuring compliance with all civil rights laws among schools and school districts. This office has specific responsibility for monitoring school district's implementation of Section 504 of the Vocational Education Act.

Peer Review   The process of subjecting research findings to scrutiny by a panel of experts who can judge the validity of claims made by a researcher. Peer review is considered a minimally necessary attribute of scientific validation. All reputable, scholarly journals subject articles to peer review prior to publication. Similarly, most respected scientific meetings require proposals to be peer reviewed.

Positive Behavioral Supports   Also referred to as *positive behavior interventions* and *supports (PBIS)*. This is a schoolwide approach to dealing with problem behaviors that employs a three-tiered set of interventions. Primary prevention strategies are designed for 80%–90% of students in the school who behave appropriately most of the time but need some basic rules and procedures to maintain order. Secondary level strategies are designed for 5%–15% of students who are at risk of more serious behavior problems and need group oriented specialized interventions. Tertiary strategies include individual strategies such as counseling and behavior plans and are targeted at 1%–7% of the students who have chronic and severe behavior problems.

Program Evaluation   The systematic collection and analysis of data for the purpose of making decisions about the value of a project or program. Evaluation research generally focuses on estimating the success in accomplishment of established program or project goals.

Proven Instructional Practices   Teaching and administrative practices that have been subjected to scientific testing and found to be consistently effective. Proven instructional practices produce the kinds of effects they claim, across many applications. Proven instructional practices have been validated by scientific studies and examined by the larger educational community.

Qualitative Research   Scientific investigation that relies on the collection of narratives in naturalistic settings through first-person observations. Qualitative research typically does not entail extensive analysis of numerical data. Inferences developed in qualitative research tend to rely on inductive rather than deductive reasoning.

Quantitative Research   Scientific investigation that entails collection of numerical data. Often quantitative research involves statistics and numerical analysis. Inferences derived from quantitative research are based on interpretation of data.

Random Error   Events or variables other than those of interest to the researcher or decision maker that affect an assessment or measurement outcome. Random error is present in all data systems, and the decision maker never knows for sure how much random error is present. Therefore, all assessment systems must include procedures to control for random error. Systems that are highly reliable are said to contain little random error.

Related Services   Defined under the IDEA as services that are provided free of charge and include transportation and such developmental, corrective, and other supportive services as may be required to assist a child with a disability to benefit from special education. Related services include various therapies, recreation and therapeutic recreation, social work and counseling services, and medical services that may be required for diagnoses or evaluation of a disability.

Reliability   The minimally essential ingredient for determining data quality. Reliability is an index of the amount of random error that an assessment system contains. Often, reliability is interpreted as relating to the stability or consistency of a test or assessment procedure. A test is reliable if it yields the same kind of results time after time.

Replication   The process of repeating studies using similar methods but different participants. Similar findings found in multiple replications are thought to be more scientifically valid than results that have been reported in only one or a few studies.

Representative Sample   A subset of the larger group about whom a researcher is interested that shares all the critical characteristics of that larger group. A sample is considered representative when observations about it can be applied validly to the larger population from which it is drawn.

Representativeness Heuristic   The mistake people commit when they make a decision on the basis of superficial or extraneous characteristics that seem to make a particular example a *representative* of the larger category.

Scientific Validation   The process of verifying the truthfulness of a theory or practice through systematic research methods. Typically, scientific validation entails publication of results in peer reviewed publications or presentation of results at scientific meetings.

Section 504   Refers to Section 504 of the 1973 Vocational Rehabilitation Act, which states that, "No qualified handicapped person shall, on the basis of handicap, be excluded from participation in, be denied the benefits of, or otherwise be subjected to discrimination under any program or activity which receives Federal financial assistance." Students with disabilities are covered under Section 504 whether or not they are found to be eligible for special education. Section 504 entitles a student to an individual accommodation plan, which is to determine what accommodations are required in instruction, setting or facilities, and assessments. Section 504 also protects the rights of adults with disabilities.

Special Education   Specially designed instruction, at no cost to parents, to meet the unique needs of a child with a disability.

Students With Disabilities   Under IDEA this includes students with "mental retardation, hearing impairments (including deafness), speech or language impairments, visual impairments (including blindness), emotional disturbance, orthopedic impairments, autism, traumatic brain injury, other health impairments, or specific learning disabilities" and who need special education and related services. Individual states can create their own categories of disability as long as they include those referred to above.

Universal Design   Designed-in flexibility to accommodate the instructional needs of many diverse learners in a single product or approach. Products and environments are designed to be usable by the largest number of people possible without the need for additional modifications beyond those incorporated into the original design. When additional adaptations are needed, they can be easily and unobtrusively accommodated by the original design.

Validity   The quality of a decision or inference that lends it credence. Validity is roughly analogous to truthfulness. While validity often is treated as an attribute inherent to tests, it is more accurate to refer to the validity of decisions based on some data or information. Validity involves both empirical data and logical reasoning. No matter how well intentioned, decisions that are based on bad data cannot be valid. For example, a well-designed assessment could be used to make poor decisions.

Index